D0093866

Garlic, an Edible Biography

CALGARY PUBLIC LIBRARY

NOV   2014

"We remember the fish, which we did eat in Egypt freely;
the cucumbers, and the melons, and the leeks,
and the onions, and the garlick."

—The Holy Bible (King James Version), Numbers 11

"And, most dear actors, eat no onions nor garlic,
for we are to utter sweet breath."

—William Shakespeare, *A Midsummer Night's Dream,* act 4, scene 2

"A nickel will get you on the subway, but garlic will get you a seat."

—Yiddish proverb

GARLIC

an Edible Biography

THE HISTORY, POLITICS, AND MYTHOLOGY
BEHIND THE WORLD'S MOST PUNGENT FOOD,
WITH OVER 100 RECIPES

Robin Cherry

ROOST BOOKS
Boston
2014

Roost Books

An imprint of Shambhala Publications, Inc.
Horticultural Hall
300 Massachusetts Avenue
Boston, Massachusetts 02115
roostbooks.com

© 2014 by Robin Cherry
Recipes by Mary Deir Donovan

All rights reserved. No part of this book may be reproduced
in any form or by any means, electronic or mechanical, including
photocopying, recording, or by any information storage and retrieval
system, without permission in writing from the publisher.

9 8 7 6 5 4 3 2 1

First Edition
Printed in the United States of America

♾ This edition is printed on acid-free paper that meets
the American National Standards Institute z39.48 Standard.
♻ This book is printed on 30% postconsumer recycled paper.
For more information please visit www.shambhala.com.
Distributed in the United States by Penguin Random House LLC
and in Canada by Random House of Canada Ltd

Designed by Lora Zorian

LIBRARY OF CONGRESS CATALOGING-IN-PUBLICATION DATA
Cherry, Robin.
Garlic, an edible biography: the history, politics, and mythology behind
the world's most pungent food: with over 100 recipes / Robin Cherry.
pages   cm
ISBN 978-1-61180-160-6 (paperback)
1. Cooking (Garlic)—History. 2. Garlic. I. Title.
TX819.G3C45 2014
641.3'526—dc23
2014007482

Contents

Garlic, an Edible Biography

INTRODUCTION

Garlic is the Lord Byron of produce, a lusty rogue that charms and seduces you but runs off before dawn, leaving a bad taste in your mouth. Yet despite its powers of seduction, garlic itself is asexual, grown from cloves without pollination. Called everything from rustic cure-all and Russian penicillin to Bronx vanilla and Italian perfume, the sulfurous bulb has permeated the history of mankind (literally) and been variously loved, worshiped, defamed, and despised. King Henry IV of France was baptized with it, and corpses were embalmed with it. It's credited with curing everything from baldness and scurvy to cancer and the plague and is one of the few products used in the world's three major ancient healing systems: Indian Ayurveda, traditional Chinese medicine, and traditional European medicine.

People throughout the world rely on garlic's powers of protection, and it's said to ward off vampires and other evil spirits, to protect babies and Belizean cab drivers, to bring luck to soldiers and jockeys, and according to Swedish farmers, to protect cows from trolls.

Sadly, garlic has also been used to discriminate against different ethnic and religious groups, especially Jews, Italians, and Koreans, and "garlic eaters" has been used as a derogatory slur for centuries. Today, with attendance at Gilroy, California's annual garlic festival topping 100,000, it's hard to think of "garlic eater" as an insult. A love for garlic has become a point of pride. You've probably never been to a carrot festival, but garlic festivals take place throughout the world from Gilroy, California, and the Hudson Valley, New York, to the Isle of Wight, United Kingdom, and Takko-Machi, Japan. Other foods may have fans; garlic has lovers.

Like many people who grew up in the 1960s and '70s, I have Julia Child to thank for introducing me to garlic. Or more precisely, I have Julia Child to thank for introducing my mother to garlic. When Child's *The French Chef* came on public television on Wednesday nights, Mom retreated to her bedroom, leaving Dad in charge of my sister and me. She closed the door and, like an eager student, scrawled notes in the margins of her new, 800-page copy of *Mastering the Art of French Cooking*. I still have the well-worn book with Mom's double check marks denoting our favorite recipes, which included Child's legendary mashed potatoes with thirty cloves of garlic. While Mom cooked her way through the book, she wore a blue and white striped apron with a red pocket that said, "Thank you, Julia Child!" I couldn't agree more.

Child would repeatedly assure her readers and viewers that they should no longer avoid garlic as something "suspiciously foreign, probably subversive, and certainly very lower-class." From her homey kitchen in Cambridge, Massachusetts, she started nothing less than a culinary revolution, rescuing garlic from its onetime confinement in old ethnic and urban communities and unleashing it on suburban kitchens throughout the country.

Mom wasn't allowed in her mother's kitchen when she was growing up, and the first time she made pasta for my father, she forgot to add water. Not wanting the same fate to befall my sister and me, she welcomed us into the kitchen. My earliest memory of cooking with garlic was to cut one clove in half and rub it on a flank steak before marinating it in soy sauce. (Today, the idea of using so little garlic seems preposterous, but revolutions don't happen overnight.)

As if making up for lost time, Mom went on to collect and comb through hundreds of cookbooks, and our breakfast room was filled with culinary inspiration courtesy of James Beard, Craig Claiborne, Paula

Peck, and Marcella Hazan (known as the Italian Julia Child), as well as all twenty-seven volumes (and accompanying spiral-bound recipe booklets) from Time-Life's still classic (but alas, out of print) *Foods of the World* series. *Foods of the World* was edited by highly regarded New York cooking teacher Michael Field, and it introduced me to lands and cuisines far from my sheltered life in suburban Cleveland, Ohio. I liked to scan my mother's collection for recipes I would use to experiment on my family. (I got paid fifty cents an hour, and cooking was my route to a new bicycle.) I started with easy recipes like pasta with Pesto alla Genovese and graduated to more exotic ones like Ciorba de Peste (Romanian Fish Soup with Garlic Sauce) from Field's *A Quintet of Cuisines*.

While garlic has always been part of my culinary repertoire, our relationship changed one day in 2004 when I discovered Georgian Fire, a spicy garlic from the former Georgian Soviet Socialist Republic.

I was in Cleveland to visit my family. My Dad was a product of the '40s and '50s and always liked the women in his life to cook. He had given me subscriptions to *Gourmet* and *Bon Appétit* when I was in college and had more time for partying and studying than Boeuf Bourguignon and Chicken Cacciatore. After my parents divorced, I gave Dad a copy of *Craig Claiborne's Kitchen Primer,* to keep him from starving as a new bachelor. He put it on a shelf and instead, got remarried to a chef.

Dad's wife, Helen, knows all the farmers at the Cleveland farmers' market so it's especially fun to go to the market with her. Although this particular visit was misty and overcast, it was brightened up by the colorful displays of lush, ripe blueberries and raspberries and boxes filled with peppery arugula and crisp green beans at the North Union Farmers Market. The market is certified as producers only, which means that you're always buying directly from the farmers themselves. Tables are lined up on both sides of The Rapid, the commuter rail line that links Cleveland's suburbs with its downtown.

I go to see regulars like super-friendly Tom Wiandt of Killbuck Valley Mushrooms, who has a degree from MIT but decided he'd rather be a fungi farmer than an engineer, and the presciently named Savery Rorimer of Snake Hill Farm, who sells amazing produce and farm-fresh eggs. But on that particular day, I noticed someone I hadn't seen be-fore—a gangly, bearded farmer in a plaid shirt and baseball cap who looked like he could be ZZ Top's country cousin. I now know it was Bill Pennell who runs Rootstown Organic Farm. Pennell stood behind a ta-ble filled with paper bags. Inside each was a single head of garlic with the garlic's name and taste description handwritten on the bag with a thick Magic Marker. These garlics were smaller than supermarket garlic and cost fifty cents each. In addition to Georgian Fire (hot, full-flavored), Pennell had Russian Red (strong, very spicy), Music (musky, mellow), and Romanian Red (strong, long-lasting).

I've been a die-hard Slavophile for years (perhaps to compensate for the indifference of my father whose family emigrated from Moldova at the turn of the twentieth century). I majored in Russian history in col-lege, and Russia is my favorite part of the world to visit. And I love, love, love spicy food. Spicy garlic from the former Soviet Union was a dream come true, although I didn't realize at the time that garlic would become a multiyear obsession that would lead me around the world from Gilroy, California, to Seoul, Korea.

As Helen is not one for moderation, we bought several bags of each garlic variety. When we got home, I sliced up one clove of each kind. The first thing I noticed when I cut into each clove was the juice. Good, fresh garlic is really juicy. Nothing like the cheap Chinese imports that clog our supermarket produce aisles.

I fell in love with the Georgian Fire. It was spicy and intense but the heat didn't diminish the awesome garlic flavor. Russian Red is also hot but it has a surprisingly sweet aftertaste. Music was, as advertised, musky with a slight tang, and Romanian Red was hot but not searing. Since garlic mellows when you cook it, the best way to use spicy garlic is raw so I decided to make Georgian Fire salsa by adapting my go-to salsa recipe. I chopped up two pounds of tomatoes, two fresh jalapeños, some cilantro, and added a splash of lime juice with two teaspoons of fresh garlic. The result was brilliant, with the two hot ingredients both complimenting and elevating the coolness of the tomatoes and cilantro.

Robin's Go-To Salsa
(Adapted from Chef Rick Bayless's Fire-Roasted Tomato Salsa)

2 lb tomatoes, diced
2 fresh jalapeño peppers, seeds removed
2 tsp fresh garlic, chopped
¼ cup cilantro, chopped
Juice from ¼ lime
Salt, to taste

Combine tomatoes, jalapeño peppers, and garlic in a food processor and pulse until you have a coarse puree. Pour into a serving dish and stir in cilantro and lime juice. Season with salt, to taste.

I became fascinated (some might say obsessed) with these exciting new garlic varieties. Suddenly, garlic had been transformed from a one-size-fits-all commodity to a kaleidoscope of flavors, colors, shapes, and sizes. I love a good research project, and I became curious about and fascinated by these new garlics. I discovered that while some of the varieties came in with Polish, German, and Italian immigrants during the late nineteenth and early twentieth centuries, most came in all at once in 1989.

The United States Department of Agriculture (USDA) had been asking the Soviet government for permission to traverse the Caucasus region and the old Silk Road to collect garlics throughout the second half of the twentieth century. Permission was always denied because the Cold War was still raging and the area was covered with Soviet missile bases. Then, in 1989, as the Soviet Union was disintegrating, the Russians invited a delegation from the USDA to come in and collect different garlic varieties. Alas, the USDA did not have enough time to set up arrangements with regional farmers to plant and harvest the garlics, so it's taken some time for them to make their away around the country.

I learned more about the garlic-collecting mission when I went to the annual convention of the Seed Savers Exchange in Decorah, Iowa, in 2009. The conference, which attracts heirloom seed preservers and aficionados, is a mellow, Midwestern affair where meals are eaten on bales of hay and people really describe German Extra Hardy garlic as "pretty dang hardy." The highlight for me was meeting John Swenson, who had actually been on the 1989 expedition.

Swenson is a retired Chicago lawyer and amateur garlic aficionado possessed with a passion for garlic. He's also the man we have to thank for bringing Pskem, Kitab, and Samarkand into the United States. Swenson and the rest of the team camped and hiked along dry riverbeds and gorges and scoured markets in Uzbekistan, Kyrgyzstan, and Tajikistan collecting garlic as they went. They were only allowed to fly at night as Swenson, also a bit of a conspiracy theorist, believes that the Soviets thought that they might be working undercover for the CIA.

I attended a presentation on growing garlic given by Joel Girardin, a bushy-bearded farmer known as the Grandfather of Minnesota Garlic. Girardin and Swenson are old friends who have lectured on garlic around the country. Once, when asked why they had such an affinity for garlic, they answered in unison, "We like to eat!" Girardin said that if you want to sell a particular kind of garlic, write "Good for Salsa" next to it. It doesn't matter what kind it is, because as Girardin proclaimed with a hearty laugh, "It's all good for salsa!"

Over the past few years, as I've delved into its long, fascinating, and sometimes sordid history, garlic has become my Scheherazade, introducing me to tales of prophets, kings, poets, and thieves. I'd be hard-pressed to name another ingredient as polarizing as garlic. People love it or hate it, but no one is ambivalent about it. This is its story.

~ Bulbs without Borders

Over the past twenty years, the hippie-esque kibbutz Neot Semadar has coaxed a surprisingly green oasis out of Israel's dusty, brown Negev desert. While touring the kibbutz, I mentioned to my guide Coby, tender of the community's vegetable garden, that I was working on a history of garlic. He immediately bounded over to his truck and pulled out two huge, rose-tinted heads of garlic that he had just harvested. "Would you like these?" "Oh my God, yes." They were spectacular.

When I landed at JFK after an exhausting flight home from Tel Aviv, I had one goal—to evade the airport's legendary Beagle Brigade. The US Customs and Border Control has trained beagles to scout out food, plants, and fellow animals for decades. Beagles were recruited as federal agents because they have an acute sense of smell and they're so cute that they don't intimidate passengers. As a result, contraband-bearing travelers are tempted to cozy up to the adorable pups, dressed in their bright green vests, and before they know it, they've been busted by Snoopy.

I heard Hailey the Beagle before I saw her. Quickly, I turned around. She was three feet away and headed right for me. I tried to hide my nervousness, but my heart was racing and beads of sweat exploded across my brow. My eyes darted around the carousel nervously. (I'd be a lousy terrorist.) Slowly, so as not to attract attention, I headed for the other side of the carousel, weaving between my fellow passengers and grateful, for the first time, that the flight from Tel Aviv had been full. Hailey and her handler followed, stopping to check on other people, but I knew she would reach me in seconds. In a flash, I dropped my carry-on on the conveyor belt. Hailey arrived just as the garlic glided away. I picked up my suitcase and headed back to the other side of the carousel to collect my contraband-containing bag. When the customs official scanned my form and ushered me on, a smile broke out across my face. Victory and garlic were mine.

Part One

THE STORY OF GARLIC

one

THE ELIXIR OF LIFE: GARLIC AND HEALTH

*Provençal cooking is based on garlic. The air in Provence
is impregnated with the aroma of garlic,
which makes it very healthful to breathe.*

—Alexandre Dumas (1802–70) *Grand Dictionnaire de Cuisine*

Garlic's health benefits have been touted throughout history, and it's been credited as a plague-beating, infection-fighting, fat-melting, parasite-killing, cholesterol-lowering, immune system–boosting, cancer-preventing, bronchitis-curing, blood pressure–controlling, impotence-treating, ringworm-healing, strength-building, mosquito-repelling pharmacopoeia that improves digestion, circulation, respiratory health, and fertility. And that's just a partial list.

Dr. Herbert Pierson, who once headed programs at the National Cancer Institute, researched folk cures and cultural eating customs that he believed offered "thousands of years worth of epidemiological evidence of the healing properties of some foods." He found garlic to be one of the most commonly referenced foods, prompting him to say, "For thousands of years, garlic had been used for the treatment and prevention of disease. So there has to be something there." Dr. Ronald Cutler, who studies alliums at the University of London, concurred but admitted that "there's tons about garlic we don't know."*

Nonetheless, tons of interesting research is taking place throughout the world, and in many cases, garlic's future looks bright, as does its ability to help us stay healthy and, when we fall sick, to get better. This section will look at garlic's healing power and potential throughout history and in contemporary culture.

GARLIC IN CLASSICAL LITERATURE AND MEDICINE

The first known mention of garlic's medical properties is in the world's oldest known medical text, a papyrus from ancient Egypt known as the Ebers Papyrus after Georg Ebers, the German Egyptologist who purchased it from an antiquities dealer in 1872. The perfectly preserved manuscript is also ancient Egypt's most complete surviving medical text. Although the Ebers Papyrus dates back to 1552 B.C.E., it's believed to have been copied from earlier texts, possibly dating back as far as 3400 B.C.E., A beautiful sixty-five-foot scroll printed in red and black hieratic (a cursive hieroglyphic style of writing), the manuscript mentions garlic as a cure for twenty-two different ailments including tumors, heart problems, headaches, skin disorders, parasites, and that medical catch-all, general malaise.

The Carlsberg Papyrus Collection, a miscellany of fragments dating back to 1200 B.C.E., was found in the temple library of the ancient Egyptian city of Tebtunis. One medical treatise includes a diagnostic test for sterility in women that both involves garlic and illustrates the connection between the medical practices of ancient Egypt and ancient Greece. The woman in question is instructed to insert a clean, peeled clove of garlic in her vagina for one night. If garlic's odor comes out of her mouth in the morning, she will bear children. It's been suggested that

---

* From the October 2009 issue of *Chemistry World,* a magazine published by Britain's Royal Society of Chemistry: http://www.rsc.org/chemistryworld/Issues/2009/October /TheSpiceofLife.asp.

blocked fallopian tubes might have prevented the garlic from reaching the mouth, but as garlic is absorbed into the skin, there's reason to believe false positives might have been the norm.

Garlic was also famed for its stamina-boosting powers, and Israelite slaves were fed garlic to keep up their strength as they built the fortified cities of Pithom and Raamses for the pharaohs. The Israelites' lack of garlic after their exodus from Egypt (1440–1400 B.C.E.) was recounted in the Old Testament of the Bible in which the desert-wandering Israelites sadly remember "the fish which we did eat in Egypt freely; the cucumbers, and the melons, and the leeks, and the onions, and the garlick."

In the Book of Ezra (one of the last books of the Old Testament, written in 400 B.C.E. after the Jews returned to Jerusalem following captivity in Babylon), the prophet decrees a specific ordinance that requires Jews to eat garlic on Friday nights (the eve of the Sabbath) because garlic served as an aid to passion and fertility and so would enhance the marital relations (i.e., sex) that couples were encouraged to enjoy as part of Jewish Sabbath observance. The Talmud (100–400 C.E.) also includes the term "garlic eater," and rabbinical literature is full of praise for garlic saying, "It satisfies hunger, it warms the body, it illuminates one's face, it increases seed, and it destroys intestinal parasites." The Jews were actually the first to call themselves garlic eaters, but unlike anti-Semites who would use it as an insult, they meant it in a good way. Use of the term "garlic eaters" as a derogatory reference to Jews dates back to ancient Rome where the Latin expression *allium olere* (stinking of garlic) was used to refer to people belonging to a low social class. Even the Roman emperor Marcus Aurelius (121–180 C.E.) referred to Jews, contemptuously, as "malodorous garlic eaters" when he returned from Palestine.

The Sages of the Talmud do offer one anti-garlic admonition: in order not to endanger one's life, one must not eat a peeled garlic clove that was left out overnight. It's believed that a "spirit of impurity" rests on the garlic clove (but only when it's peeled and left out overnight). It's unclear that there was ever any scientific basis for this injunction and it's omitted from later legal decrees. Some rabbis claimed that this "spirit of impurity" was no longer widespread in their time. Others had never even heard of it. If even a minuscule part of the garlic is left unpeeled, or if it is cooked, mixed with other ingredients, or left out for just part of the night, the prohibition is lifted. Furthermore, one who eats the garlic and dies will be judged by the Heavenly Court as a person who took his or her own life, a serious crime as suicide is forbidden under Jewish law.

THE MYTHICAL CURE

In Greek mythology, Asclepius, son of the god Apollo, was taught about healing herbs by the wise centaur, Chiron. He became so skilled that he was even able to raise the dead, which did not sit well with Hades, God of the Underworld. Hades complained to Zeus, who was also displeased to see Asclepius tampering with the natural order of things, so Zeus killed Asclepius with a thunderbolt while he was in the middle of writing down the formula for immortality. Seeing that Asclepius was writing something, Zeus sent down a pouring rain to destroy the paper. It melted into the earth, and when the sun came out, a plant sprang up where the formula had fallen. That plant was, of course, garlic, leading some to conclude that garlic was in the formula for immortality. Asclepius had several children who followed him into medicine, including his daughters Hygieia (the goddess of health from whose name we got the word *hygiene*) and Panacea (the goddess of universal remedy from whose name comes the term *panacea,* meaning "cure-all").

In ancient Rome, garlic's healing properties were acclaimed by both Hippocrates, considered the father of modern medicine, and Dioscorides, the father of modern pharmacology. Hippocrates, who founded the first school of medicine focused on treating the causes of disease rather than just its symptoms, famously said, "Let food be thy medicine and medicine be thy food." He prescribed garlic for a variety of conditions, including pulmonary disease and tumors, and as a cleansing agent. In *De materia medica* (first century C.E.), one of the most important herbal books of all time, Dioscorides recommends garlic to clean the arteries. This thinking was revolutionary at the time as it was believed that the arteries transferred air through the body while blood was transported exclusively through the veins. By suggesting that one's cardiovascular health could be improved by eating garlic, Dioscorides foreshadowed studies that continue to this day. He also recommended garlic to prevent gastrointestinal disorders, to alleviate joint disease and seizures, and to treat bites from both mad dogs and vipers, as well as a cure for asthma, black eyes, baldness, birthmarks, and lice. *De materia medica* was widely used throughout Europe until the 1600s.

As ancient Rome overtook ancient Greece as the world's superpower, the medical traditions of Greece transferred to Rome. Although Dioscorides was Greek, as the leading medical practitioner of the day, he was appointed to serve as head physician for Emperor Nero's army. In addition to being a longtime fan of Greek culture, Nero was also a big garlic fan and is even credited with inventing aioli, the legendary garlic mayonnaise that's now synonymous with Provence. Nero ruled during the three-century-long Pax Romana, a time during which Pliny the Elder said that Provence "was more than a province, it was another Italy."

A contemporary of Dioscorides, Pliny the Elder was the great Roman naturalist who wrote the encyclopedia *Historia naturalis,* in which he devoted a whole chapter to garlic, recommending it for sixty-one different disorders and believing that it offered protection against toxins and infections and cured consumption (the archaic name for tuberculosis). He also wrote of Egyptians invoking garlic as a deity when taking an oath and as an aphrodisiac when pounded with coriander in wine. Mindful of this, the Romans would have garlic amulets or wreathes at their infamous orgies so that the garlic could be used to invigorate those participants in need of a little pick-me-up. In addition to its use as a remedy for human maladies, Pliny wrote, "Beasts of burden, it is said, will void their urine all the more easily, and without any pain, if the genitals are rubbed with garlic." It's hard not to wonder how, and by whom, this was first discovered.

In the second century C.E., the Roman physician and philosopher Galen declared garlic the most popular folk remedy of the day and prescribed it for so many maladies that he christened it *theriaca rusticorum,* meaning cure-all for the poor. As a physician to the gladiators, Galen treated wounded warriors with bandages soaked in garlic juice. He claimed that no gladiator under his care had ever died, and although this claim is spurious, his reputation earned him the appointment as personal physician to Emperor Marcus Aurelius and his two successors.

THE SPICE ROUTE

The evolution of traditional Chinese medicine (TCM) parallels the development of medicine in ancient Egypt. Recognition of garlic's medicinal benefits within TCM dates back to 2600 B.C.E. when an emperor recognized its miraculous properties as an antidote to poison. The Yellow Emperor, Huang-ti, now revered as a legendary sovereign and cultural leader, is the father of Chinese medical knowledge. His medical discoveries laid out the foundations for the principles of TCM, which were later written down in the *Huang-ti nei ching* (*The Yellow Emperor's Classic of Medicine*).

It's said that Huang-ti was out walking with his followers when they all stopped to eat the leaves of the *yu-yu,* a fruit that turned out to be poisonous and made everyone quite sick. Huang-ti noticed some wild garlic growing nearby, and at his urging, he and his companions ate the garlic and all were cured. This prompted the emperor to introduce the garlic bulb into cultivation. (It was a rollicking success as today China is the largest garlic producer in the world thanks to its low production costs and high domestic demand.) The therapeutic uses of garlic in TCM are numerous; it was prescribed for aiding respiration and digestion, treating diarrhea and worm infestation, and combating depression, fatigue, headaches, and insomnia.

Garlic's "warmth" is believed to increase the temperature of an infected area, creating an inhospitable environment for harmful organisms. This warmth is also believed to encourage the body to dissolve masses of stagnation, which is how cancer is described in TCM. Stagnation is said to be caused by coldness in the body, so it's believed that by warming the body with garlic, you melt the stagnation and allow natural enery or life force (qi) to move freely. As elsewhere in the ancient world, doctors prescribed garlic for men with "intimacy problems," but TCM's earliest pharmacopoeia, *Shen nung pen ts'ao ching* (*The Divine Husbandman's Classic of Materia Medica*), prohibited the consumption of garlic by Buddhist priests and those who were fasting.

The Chinese introduced garlic to their Korean neighbors, and it was, to put it mildly, a sensation. Today, the Koreans are the world's largest per capita consumers of garlic, eating a staggering twenty-two pounds a year owing to their passion for garlicky kimchi. (In contrast, the average American consumes a paltry two and a half pounds a year.)

Garlic and mugwort were Korea's first recorded medicinal herbs thanks to their role in the country's founding myth, the Legend of T'angun, in which twenty cloves of garlic and a bear-woman are credited with the creation of the country. It's said that God sent his son to earth to build a peaceful kingdom and be its king. One day, a tiger and a bear, who observed the happy and civilized lives of man, went to the king and asked him to reincarnate them in human form. The king gave them twenty cloves of garlic and a handful of bitter mugwort and told them to go into a cave to pray. He told them, "If you eat these and do not see sunlight for one hundred days you will become human beings." The impatient tiger gave up and returned to the wild, but the bear prayed and emerged as a woman. After some time as a human, she asked God for a child of her own. The king, touched by her prayers, transformed himself, temporarily, into a man, married her, and they had a son, T'angun. T'angun succeeded his father as king and became the founding father of Korea. Thus Korea was born, and garlic and mugwort became the country's first recorded medical herbs.

The Koreans introduced garlic to the Japanese, and while it didn't take as a culinary item for a few centuries, garlic's medicinal properties were incorporated into Kampo, Japan's botanical medical system. Kampo is based on TCM but has a strong focus on the study and use of medicinal herbs. Kampo medicine is integrated into Japan's national health care system and taught in Japanese medical schools. Garlic is considered so powerful that it's designated as a drug in Japan.

Traveling a more southerly road from China's Tien Shan mountains, garlic's entrance to India probably coincided with its arrival in China. Garlic's importance in the healing process in India goes back to the three ancient medical traditions (Siddha, Ayurveda, and Unani), all of which made extensive use of garlic. Siddha, which dates back to the sixth or seventh century B.C.E., is one of the world's oldest medical systems; its junior sibling is the 2,000-year-old Ayurveda (often tranlated as "science of life"). Both prescribe garlic to maintain a healthy heart and purify the blood.

Garlic figures prominently in one of the oldest known treatises on Ayurvedic medicine, a collection of Sanskrit writings on birch bark known as the Bower Manuscript after the British intelligence officer who purchased it in 1890. Bower bought the manuscript (which now resides at the Bodleian Library at Oxford University) from a local resident in Kuqa, a Silk Road trading town.

The document's first treatise, which dates to the first half of the sixth century C.E., is about garlic's mythical beginnings in India. Legend says that when Lord Vishnu was distributing nectar to the demigods, two demons named Rahu and Ketu sat in line to receive the nectar. By mistake, Vishnu poured nectar into their mouths. Almost at once, he was informed that these two were demons and he cut off their heads before the nectar had passed through their throats. The nectar fell on the ground, and in the place where it spilled, garlic and onion sprouted. For that reason, Indians consider garlic and onions a nectar but not one that is fit for Lord Vishnu as it touched the mouth of demons. In Ayurveda, it's said that garlic and onions still act like nectar in curing diseases—but when people eat garlic, their body will be very strong like the demon's body, yet their intelligence will be compromised like that of demons.

In the Bower Manuscript, garlic is called "the universal remedy" and prescribed for infections, parasites, weakness and fatigue, and a variety of digestive disturbances. The manuscript includes recipes for garlic juice, crushed garlic, fried garlic, garlic and meat, and garlic and barley balls. It also includes the brilliant ruse, Garlic Purified through a Cow, which states: "When a cow has been waiting for three nights with almost no grass, one should give her a preparation of two parts grass to one part garlic stalks. A Brahmin can then partake of her milk, curds, ghee, or even buttermilk, and banish various diseases while maintaining propriety." The Bower Manuscript also describes a garlic festival during which the rooftops, gateways, and upper windows of the local houses were hung with garlands of garlic and residents draped themselves with wreathes of garlic and worshiped garlic in their courtyards.

Garlic is also mentioned in the Sanskrit medical treatise Charaka-Samhita, the best-known work of Ayurveda, which was relied on from the second century B.C.E. to the second century C.E. Charaka, the father of traditional Indian medicine, recommended garlic as a diuretic, heart stimulant, and digestive aid as well as for the treatment of heart disease, eye ailments, and arthritis. He felt so strongly about its power, he wrote, "But for its unpleasant odor, garlic would be costlier than gold." Ayurvedic medicine also advocates the use of garlic for the prevention and cure of cholera, colic, dysentery, hardening of the arteries, tuberculosis, and typhoid.

Mindful of garlic's aphrodisiacal properties, however, Indian monks, widows, and adolescents are expected to refrain from eating it to ensure that their sexual urges are not stimulated. In the Brahma Net Sutra, a precept forbids any disciple of the Buddha from eating the five pungent herbs—garlic, chives, leeks, onions, and asafetida—even if they are added as flavoring to other dishes. Those following the Jain religion do not eat garlic because it's viewed as a food that creates anger and excitement and because in the practice of ahimsa (their philosophy of nonviolence), it's believed that consuming a garlic bulb's many individual cloves, or souls, would destroy souls that could possibly produce many more living things. While Jains will not use garlic at all, Brahmins permit its medicinal use.

India's third medical tradition, Unani (the Arabic spelling of "Ionian"), refers to the ancient Greek medicinal system that evolved in the

Muslim world over the last thirteen centuries. The tradition was promoted by the great Islamic physician Avicenna ("Ibn Sina" in Arabic), who built upon the teachings of Hippocrates and Galen. In Unani medicine, garlic is used to treat everything from paralysis and colic to ulcers and forgetfulness. In addition to *rason*, garlic is also known by another Sanskrit name, *mahanshadha*, which translates as "panacea."

THE BEST WAY TO POSTPONE SENILITY AND DEATH

The fall of the Roman Empire in 476 C.E. signified the end of antiquity and the beginning of the Dark Ages, which cast a shroud over Europe from the fifth to tenth century. Although most of Europe was experiencing a dark period, a golden age of Islamic culture flourished from the eighth to the twelfth century when Muslims in Andalusia, the Middle East, and North Africa studied and improved upon the work of the ancient Greeks and made significant advances in medicine, science, and cuisine.

One of the reasons for the advances in medicine was that the prophet Mohammed, who founded the religion of Islam in 610 C.E., told his followers that "Allah never inflicts a disease unless he makes a cure for it." This encouraged early Muslim scholars to look to botanical and other natural products for medical cures. Mohammed also posited that a plant's appearance gives clues to its medicinal uses. In *The Medicine of the Prophet*, he recommends using garlic, a plant with many sections and legs (resembling an insect), as a poultice for scorpion bites and bee stings. He said that "although onion and garlic have a bad smell, they are cures for seventy different illnesses that cannot be cured by any other means." Meanwhile in Europe, during medieval times, Christian monks were keeping the knowledge of the medical use of therapeutic plants alive. The monks would copy and recopy ancient Greek, Roman, and Arab medical documents. Dioscorides's *De materia medica* remained an important reference, and garlic continued to be prized for its medicinal properties. Monks were the gardeners and healers of the day and grew garlic in their monastery gardens, unlike those religious leaders who had banned garlic from their institutions. One of the leading medical books of the day was even a prayer book, *Hortulus animae* (*Little Garden of the Soul*), which also highlighted the utilitarian value of the garden. Its preface notes, "A tiny garden will often produce a variety of salutary herbs of which medicine knows the value." Garlic was featured extensively and was specifically prescribed for people with leprosy. As a result, lepers became known as *pilgarlics* because they had to peel their heads of garlic themselves. *Pilgarlic* became a generic term for anyone who appeared pitiful and later to describe a bald man. Originally, the association with baldness came from the belief that syphilis caused a man's hair to fall out; therefore, he should be scorned. Once the connection between hair loss and venereal disease was disproved, the term came to connote a man whose head is as smooth as a peeled clove of garlic.

The dispensary of a Benedictine monastery evolved into the Medical School at Salerno, which became the most important center of medical learning from the tenth to the thirteenth century. Salerno was a popular health resort dating back to the days of the Roman emperors. The school was notable for integrating the medical traditions of the ancient Greeks and Romans with those of the Arabs and the Jews. During this time, medical poems written in Latin were a popular way to convey information to people in an easy-to-understand way, and these remain an important source of medical literature. One of the most famous is a twelfth-century medical poem from Salerno called "Regimen sanitatis Salernitanum" ("A Regimen of Health from Salerno"). In it, garlic's virtues are extolled, albeit in a somewhat backhanded way:

> Since Garlic hath powers to save from death,
> Bear with it though it make unsavory breath:
> And scorn not Garlic, like some that think
> It only makes men wink, and drink, and stink.

In medieval Germany, garlic was cited in the concept of the four humors and the doctrine of signatures. The ancient concept of the four humors (melancholy, choler, phlegm, and blood) was used to explain human constitutions and goes back to the times of Hippocrates and Galen. St. Hildegard von Bingen, a leading German physician and mystic who practiced during the latter part of the twelfth century, was one of its major adherents. St. Hildegard gave garlic a prominent role in her medical works and came to the conclusion that garlic ought to be eaten raw, claiming it lost its strength when it was cooked, presumably because raw garlic is more pungent. She said that an angel told her to mix garlic with hyssop to cure asthma, to mix it with the herb heal-all for bloody coughs, and to mix it with lavender blossoms and comfrey leaves for tuberculosis. Unable to write, St. Hildegard dictated her visions to a monk.

Another ancient belief, previously cited by the prophet Mohammed, was that God placed plants on earth for the benefit of mankind. It was christened the Doctrine of Signatures by Jacob Boehme, a German shoemaker who had a mystical vision of the relationship between God and man. In his seventeenth-century work *Signatura rerum* (The Signature of All Things), he wrote that fruits and vegetables give clues to their medicinal powers. For example, a walnut resembles a brain and so is good for brain health; a leaf that is good for the liver is shaped like a liver; and so on. Other interpreters of the Doctrine of Signatures believe, in addition to the cure for insect bites, the phallic appearance of a head of garlic recommends it as an aphrodisiac, while the windpipe nature of the stalk indicates its usefulness in treating respiratory ailments.

The Renaissance brought a heightened interest in herbal remedies and the medicinal properties of plants. In Italy, "physic" gardens were set up at major universities to grow plants of medicinal value, and garlic was included as one of the "simples," those plants that didn't require additives to provide medical benefit. These precursors to today's botanical gardens were established in Italy, at the universities of Pisa, Padua, Florence, and Bologna, before spreading throughout Europe.

In England, this renewed interest in plant-based remedies combined with the invention of the printing press and the introduction of new plants from the recently "discovered" Americas led to an increase in the publication of herbals and cookbooks. During this time we also see the schism between garlic as a food and garlic as a medicine in England. This rift is well illustrated in two of the most important English herbals written by botanist John Gerard and John Parkinson, apothecary to James I and later royal botanist to Charles I.

In *The Herball, or Generall Historie of Plantes* (1597), a heavily illustrated, 1,480-page doorstop of a book, Gerard claims that garlic "yeeldeth [sic] to the body no nourishment at all" yet prescribes it for a variety of ailments including sore throats, coughs, colds, poison, worms, and the bites of venomous animals. Parkinson's herbal is called *Paradisi in sole paradisus terrestris* (1629), and in it, Parkinson echoes the words of Galen, calling garlic "the poor man's Treacle, that is a remedy for all diseases." When it comes to food, he writes, "Our dainty age refuses them in all sorts but the poorest." (*Paradisi,* the first word in the title, comes from the old Iranian word meaning "park," and the title is a pun meaning "Park-in-Sun's Earthly Paradise.")

Several English writers composed new herbals using the work of the ancients and monks as a foundation but adding their own observations. As an example, in *The Art of Simpling* (1657), William Coles seconds the ancient Greek belief that "cocks having eaten Garlick, are most stout to fight and so are horses." But then, Coles goes on to add his own tip: planting garlic in mole-infested gardens will cause the pesky rodents to "leap out of the ground presently." (It turns out that both moles and gophers dislike garlic's sulfuric compounds and garlic does indeed encourage them to relocate.)

Francis Bacon, the influential philosopher, statesman, and scientist, advocated the medical use of garlic (and opium) in his *Historia vitae et mortis,* written in 1623. Bacon claimed that "the way to postpone senility and death is to see to it that the spirits are dense and consequently have a gentle heat that will not dry up and eventually destroy the body. Ways of condensing the spirit are: take opium, breathe cold air, smell fresh earth. Ways of keeping it gently warm are: to eat garlic."

Garlic, with its antibacterial, antifungal, and antiviral properties, was eaten to ward off the plague. A seventeenth-century writer even said, "Our doctor is a clove of garlic." Doctors (of the human variety)

⌒ Insect Repellent of Epic Proportion

Thanks to garlic, Spanish immigrants were more likely to survive in the New World than their English, Dutch, and French counterparts. To endure the heat, settlers from the Old World wore clothing made of layers of linen under heavy wool coats. When they perspired, the linen would absorb their body moisture and the wool coats would insulate them. This was early American wicking. The wool coats would also hold the moisture in, creating natural air-conditioning. Adding insult to perspiration, none of the European settlers bathed regularly. They all smelled horrible, but only the Spaniards ate tons of garlic, and as a result, they exuded the smell of garlic, which repelled disease-carrying mosquitoes.

carried garlic cloves in their pockets when visiting patients, and grave diggers who buried the dead drank wine spiked with crushed raw garlic. French priests who ate a lot of garlic could visit their congregants with greater security, while the garlic-averse English clergy often caught the infection and succumbed to the disease. Garlic was also used to soothe victims of the disease; after the swelling was lanced, a warm poultice of garlic, onion, and butter was applied. Garlic was also a major ingredient in Four Thieves' Vinegar, a protection against the plague, so named because during an outbreak in Marseilles in 1726, four thieves who were arrested for robbing corpses credited their immunity to wearing masks soaked in garlic, vinegar, and herbs. Today, people who practice Hoodoo use Four Thieves' Vinegar to protect themselves from illness, psychic attacks, and troublesome people. To banish a troublesome person, one is advised to pour a bottle of Four Thieves' Vinegar on the person's door or porch while cursing them and telling them where to go. (One should probably avoid doing this when the neighbors are around.)

Plague doctors were hired to visit victims of the plague to verify that they had been afflicted. They wore heavy, ankle-length, waxed leather overcoats, wide-brimmed hats, and masks with rounded glass eye coverings and a cone shaped like a beak. (Their otherworldly appearance was so terrifying that if the disease didn't kill you, the sight of the plague doctor might.) The beak was filled with garlic and herbs to purify the air that the doctors breathed (and to protect them from the noxious fumes given off by decomposing corpses). The doctors also carried a stick that could be used to examine a patient without direct contact or to push away patients who got too close. Herbalists recommended that people press a garlic clove to the nostrils before entering the unsanitary streets to protect themselves against "the noxious wastes that could enter the nostrils." Nostradamus, better known for his prophesies, was a plague doctor who was well regarded for his garlic-aloe anti-plague formula. (Garlic's antibacterial action was supplemented by aloe's immune-boosting effects.)

FRIEND TO THE AFFLICTED

Crossing the pond, we find an indigenous wild garlic (*allium canadense*) that was used by the Native Americans who inhabited the country long before Christopher Columbus introduced cultivated garlic to the so-called New World in 1492. Juice from wild garlic was applied directly to wounds and burns and made into a poultice for treating boils. Garlic was also used to soothe bee stings, insect bites, and snake bites, and cooked garlic juice was dissolved into maple sugar and used as both a cough syrup and a treatment for hives.

While the early settlers brought over their medical practices from Europe, some wisely drew on the Native Americans' use of herbal remedies. One was John Tennent, a Virginia doctor who published the first American medical self-help manual, *Every Man his own Doctor: or the Poor Planter's Physician,* in 1727. Tennent's work was considered controversial for its exclusion of the popular remedies of the day—mercury, opium, and quinine—in favor of Native American herbal remedies. His treatment for gravel (as kidney stones were then known) was to drink cider mixed with wild garlic juice every morning and night for a week.

America's early explorers also used wild garlic. The French missionary Jacques Marquette, who founded Michigan's first European settlement, listed wild garlic as an important source of food on his expeditions, and the physician who accompanied American explorers Lewis and Clark noted their expedition team's use of wild garlic to control scurvy. Historical records show that European settlers relied on indigenous plants that were closely related to those they remembered from the "old country," so it's not surprising that wild garlic was used as garlic had been since ancient times to treat fevers, skin irritations, hemorrhoids, earaches, rheumatism, arthritis, parasites, blood disorders, and lung problems.

Returning to cultivated garlic, the cargo manifest of Columbus's caravel *Niña* included "12 pannier-baskets of salt pork and one pannier-basket of garlic which all weighs 2,450 pounds." Columbus was an Italian, though he sailed under the Spanish crown, and the Spaniard explorers who followed him brought garlic and many other staples from Spain with them. The Spanish explorers introduced garlic to Mexico, and from there, it spread to the neighboring countries of Central America and South America where it became an essential ingredient in the region's cuisine.

Despite the appreciation for garlic's medical benefits in early America, its potent aroma did nothing to endear it to the early Puritan settlers as the first cookbook written by an American attests. Published in 1798, it was given the spectacular title of *American Cookery, or The Art of Dressing Viands, Fish, Poultry and Vegetables, and the Best Modes of Making Pastes, Puffs, Pies, Tarts, Puddings, Custards and Preserves, and All Kinds of Cakes. . . . Adapted to this Country and All Grades of Life by Amelia Simmons, an American Orphan.* The author expressed the prevailing view of garlic in America when she asserted, "Garlicks, tho' used by the French, are better adapted to the uses of medicine than cookery."

Simmons's sentiment held sway, by and large, for the next 150 years. The Shakers, the small monastic religious community best known today for their graceful furniture, were devoted to hard work and known to have the best medicinal gardens in the country. Drawing on the herbal knowledge of Native Americans, they were one of the first groups to grow, dry, and sell medicinal herbs and are credited with launching the

American medicinal herb industry in 1799. They used and recommended garlic as a treatment for respiratory diseases.

The most popular nineteenth-century American medical book was *Gunn's Domestic Medicine, or Poor Man's Friend in the Hours of Affliction, Pain and Sickness* published by Dr. John Gunn of Knoxville, Tennessee, in 1830. The book was later adapted and published as *Gunn's New Domestic Physician: Or, Home Book of Health* in 1878. That edition featured garlic prominently as a diuretic; an antidote for earaches, fevers, worms, and kidney stones; and a treatment for asthma and other pulmonary disorders. Gunn was also an enthusiastic advocate for the use of opium, and his treatment for whooping cough was the juice of garlic sweetened with honey or a teaspoonful of sweet oil to which one might add a few drops of paregoric (camphorated tincture of opium) or laudanum (tincture of opium). Unfortunately, as laudanum contained twenty-five times more opium than paregoric, confusion led to overdose and death in several patients.

Gunn's work foreshadowed the rise of the Eclectic movement, medical based primarily on the use of herbal remedies that were popular in North America from the 1880s to the 1930s. One of the most respected Eclectic practitioners was John King, who published *American Dispensatory* in 1877. King recommended garlic as a stomach tonic that was also useful for treating coughs, hoarseness, and worms. He also recommended blending garlic juice, almond oil, and glycerin for deafness and earaches. King also cautioned that "if garlic is used too freely or if one's system is especially excited, it might cause flatulence, stomach irritation, hemorrhoids, headache, and fever."

The first attempt to promote uniformity in medicines was the *U.S. Pharmacopeia* (USP), first published in 1820. Initially designed as a compendium of recipes for the best and most established medicines, the USP evolved into list of quality standards. Garlic was included in the list of official ingredients from the beginning. In 1888, the American Pharmaceutical Association published its first *National Formulary of Unoficinal* [sic] *Preparations* (NF). Garlic was not included in the NF until 1906 when it included a preparation for a garlic syrup that was recommended for people with pulmonary diseases. (The elixirs in the first edition of the NF made heavy use of strychnine, morphine, opium, and alcohol and included such unusual ingredients as iron wire, Irish moss, and hog pancreas.)

After the depression of the 1890s, immigrants flocked to America, and increasingly, they came from the garlic-loving countries of eastern and southern Europe. When the 1918 influenza outbreak ravaged the globe, killing 600,000 people in the United States and 50 million worldwide, some of these immigrants burned garlic in their homes, allowing the fumes to waft through the air in what many historians record as successful attempts to ward off the disease. Desperate to combat the epidemic, many people, both immigrants and not, turned to folk remedies, and survivors recalled wearing muslin bags of garlic or strings of garlic cloves around their necks. At the peak of the epidemic, the *Boston Globe* published an influenza cure that called for blending a poultice of three pounds of onions and one pound of garlic. The poultice was then to be applied "to the feet, under the knees, and around the neck of the patient every three or four hours." Thanks to the increased interest in garlic, garlic prices shot up dramatically.

Garlic was also called on to save soldiers during both World Wars. During WWI, the British government asked its citizens to supply as much garlic as they could, most of which was used as an antiseptic to treat wounded soldiers. Garlic was so important that the government paid one shilling a pound, roughly fifteen dollars in today's currency. Army doctors would blend raw garlic juice with water and apply it to soldiers' wounds with swabs of sterilized sphagnum moss.

Between the two wars, British bacteriologist Alexander Fleming accidentally discovered the bacteria-killing mold, penicillin, in 1928. (Fleming was a brilliant scientist who kept a notoriously messy lab.) He had left a pile of dirty petri dishes in a corner when he went on vacation, and when he got back, discovered that one of his dishes of staphylococcus culture was contaminated with a blue-green mold that appeared to inhibit the growth of bacteria. This discovery pushed garlic into the background as a folksy cure-all and doctors prescribed penicillin to cure infections. During WWII, however, there wasn't enough penicillin to treat the legions of injured Red Army soldiers and garlic was back in business, earning the sobriquet "Russian penicillin." As a missionary in Africa in the 1950s, Dr. Albert Schweitzer used garlic to treat cholera, dysentery, and typhus.

⟜ Russian Remedy

Garlic vodka is a popular antiflu remedy in Russia. To make it, finely chop a bulb of garlic and add it to a pint of vodka. Stir the drink twice a day and allow it to infuse for at least twenty-one days. This is not a beverage but a medicine, and it's recommended that those afflicted take ten to twenty drops of garlic vodka, twice a day.

Another popular cold remedy is garlic-honey syrup. (Honey soothes the throat and reduces coughing.) Chop up a whole bulb of garlic and place it in a glass jar. Cover it with half a cup of raw honey. Let it sit for at least three but preferably twenty-four hours. Take one teaspoon of the syrup every hour, as needed. (If the syrup is too strong for your taste, add some soy sauce and you have a lovely marinade for chicken or meat.)

THE SCIENCE BEHIND THE CURE

We know now that most of garlic's medicinal benefits are derived from sulfur-bearing compounds that are also responsible for its characteristic odor and taste. While, as we've seen, garlic's healing properties have been touted for millennia, it wasn't until the middle of the nineteenth century that researchers understood the science behind them. In 1844, Austrian chemist Theodor Wertheim used steam distillation to extract an organic sulfur compound from raw garlic. He named it allyl sulfur and attributed garlic's therapeutic properties to what he called "the evil-smelling oil." (Wertheim had incorrectly identified the compound as diallyl sulfide, a flavor compound but not the compound responsible for most of garlic's beneficial attributes. The actual compound, diallyl disulfide, was correctly identified by another German scientist, F. W. Semmler, in 1892.)

Meanwhile, in 1858 in France, chemist and microbiologist Louis Pasteur was the first scientist to document that garlic has the ability to inhibit the growth of bacteria. Pasteur placed cloves of garlic in a petri dish full of bacteria. A few days later, he noticed that a bacteria-free area surrounded each clove. Pasteur's work led to the initiation of thousands of subsequent studies that continue to this day.

In 1944 came another first as American chemist Chester Cavallito became the first scientist to isolate and study allicin, a sulfur compound that's not present in garlic until it's cut or crushed. Cavallito's pioneering work earned him the title "Father of Garlic Chemistry." Four years later, Arnold Stoll and Ewald Seebeck, researchers at the Swiss pharmaceutical company Sandoz, showed that intact garlic doesn't contain allicin at all. It possesses a related substance, alliin, which is converted into allicin when it comes in contact with alliinase, an enzyme located in neighboring cells. Stoll's and Seebeck's discovery made it possible to produce allicin synthetically, and although the scientists knew that allicin could kill bacteria, the two men were told to abandon further research because Sandoz's board of directors didn't believe that anyone would take allicin to treat infections because of its offensive odor.

Allicin, the substance produced when garlic is crushed or "injured," is garlic's natural defense mechanism against insects and fungi. Researchers now know that allicin is highly unstable and breaks down almost at once. In this process, however, allicin breaks down into more than one hundred biologically active sulfur-containing compounds, some of which may offer as yet unknown therapeutic properties.

One of these chemical compounds is ajoene. Ajoene, which was isolated and synthesized by chemist Dr. Eric Block and his colleagues in 1984, is the chemical most responsible for garlic's anticoagulant (blood clotting) properties, meaning it may reduce the risk of heart disease and stroke. It also has powerful antimicrobial properties that help prevent yeast infections and treat fungal infections. Block named ajoene (*ajo* is Spanish for "garlic") to honor his colleagues in Venezuela.

A CLOVE OF PREVENTION: GARLIC AND
TWENTY-FIRST-CENTURY MEDICAL RESEARCH

In addition to being antibacterial, garlic is antifungal, antiparasitic, and antiviral. While antibiotics should be used for life-threatening infections, garlic's sustained properties are ideally suited for nonacute (but really, really uncomfortable) yeast infections (including diaper rash) and fungal infections like ringworm, jock itch, and athlete's foot.

Raw garlic (along with pumpkin seeds, pomegranates, beets, and carrots) is a good way to rid the body of intestinal parasites. And anyone who's struggled to fight off a lingering head cold or miserable flu knows that antibiotics are powerless against viral infections. In addition to preventing colds, garlic is effective in killing viral meningitis, viral pneumonia, influenza, and herpes.

Although garlic is not as powerful as pharmaceutical antibiotics, it does have some benefits that could be especially valuable at a time when we're facing the specter of antibiotic-resistant superbugs (brought on by the overprescription and overuse of antibiotics). Unlike penicillin, for example, garlic is a broad-spectrum antibiotic, meaning it's effective against a wide range of disease-causing bacteria. Antibiotics, on the other hand, are designed to kill a narrow range of germs.

Garlic also kills bacteria directly by invading their cells and causing them to explode; thus bacteria have no opportunity to develop a resistance to it. Pharmaceutical antibiotics, on the other hand, kill bacteria indirectly, frequently leaving behind cells that are genetically unaffected by the drug. These cells multiply, and over time, the infection becomes completely immune to the antibiotic. Thus, as a result of our repeated use of pharmaceutical antibiotics, the drugs that were created to kill the disease promote the development of bacteria that are resistant to it. Alexander Fleming, himself, foresaw this problem and issued a warning on antibiotic resistance in his 1945 Nobel Prize acceptance speech.

Several powerful antibiotic-resistant infections are currently creating grave concern among scientists throughout the world. Each year, roughly

2 million people develop these infections and 23,000 die from them. The rise of antibiotic-resistant infections prompted Dr. Arjun Srinivasan, associate director of the US Centers for Disease Control and Prevention (CDC), to declare that "the age of antibiotics has come to an end." The doctor said that humans and livestock have been overmedicated to such a degree that bacteria are now resistant to antibiotics. While this is bad news for the pharmaceutical industry, it could be a boon for complementary and alternative medicine practitioners—and garlic growers.

Garlic shows promise against two of the three most dangerous bacterial infections (christened "nightmare superbugs" by the CDC): antibiotic-resistant gonorrhea and MRSA (methicillin-resistant Staphylococcus aureus, commonly found in hospitals where it has the potential to weaken those whose immune systems are already compromised).

Garlic's antibacterial properties might also help to prevent food poisoning by killing the bacteria from E. coli, salmonella, and campylobacter, all three of which are deemed a "serious threat" (a notch below nightmare superbug) by the CDC. An exciting new study from Washington State University found that not only was garlic one hundred times more effective than both erythromycin and ciprofloxacin at killing campylobacter, it often worked much faster than the two antibiotics. Perhaps one of the problems our society faces vis-à-vis antibiotic overuse is demonstrated by this statement on the Mayo Clinic's website in reference to treating one of the other nightmare superbugs, C. difficile: "Ironically, the standard treatment for C. difficile is another antibiotic."

Garlic Supplements

Wakunaga, a pharmaceutical company based in Hiroshima, Japan, introduced Kyolic, tablets of odorless, aged garlic extract, in 1955. Kyolic was developed by a German doctor assigned to prevent the overuse of antibiotics in postwar Japan. The doctor thought that garlic, with its antibiotic properties, could be used to improve and maintain the health of the Japanese people, especially those who had suffered atomic radiation. He discovered that aging garlic causes it to both lose its odor and increase its healing properties. By eliminating the odor, Wakunaga claims to have created a "sociable garlic." The supplement is said to support healthy cholesterol levels already in a normal range, circulation, immune function, liver function, and nerves, and it assists in fighting stress and fatigue. Kyolic's competitors claim that aged garlic lacks allicin, the compound that makes garlic beneficial. Wakunaga concedes that Kyolic does not contain allicin but claims that aging produces two sulfuric compounds that provide higher antioxidant activity than both fresh garlic and other commercial supplements.

Cardiovascular Health

Heart disease is the leading cause of death in the United States, killing 600,000 people a year. In evaluating garlic's role in boosting cardiovascular health and preventing heart disease, studies suggest that garlic is most beneficial in reducing blood pressure and slowing down the progression of atherosclerosis (hardening of the arteries).

A recent review of twenty-one studies conducted on humans concludes that garlic supplements can reduce blood pressure by up to 10 percent by helping red blood cells produce hydrogen sulfide, which helps to relax the blood vessels and control blood pressure. Research on hydrogen sulfide has been so promising that some scientists think it might be the next big thing in anti-aging. Insufficient levels of hydrogen sulfide in the blood are associated with Alzheimer's and Parkinson's diseases. This thinking presents a dramatic reversal as the malodorous, rotten egg–smelling gas was used as a chemical weapon during WWI.

Garlic also acts as a blood thinner, which may help prevent heart attacks and strokes. As mentioned earlier, ajoene is the compound most responsible for garlic's anticlotting properties. Garlic plays a role comparable to—and some say superior to—that of aspirin in thinning blood (and it tastes better unless you fondly remember chalky orange St. Joseph baby aspirin). Garlic is also well tolerated in most individuals, while conventional hypertensive drugs have a long list of possible side effects.

Research on garlic's role in reducing cholesterol—specifically LDL (low-density lipoprotein) or "bad" cholesterol—is inconclusive. LDL circulating in the blood at high levels can build up and clog the arteries. If a clot forms in a narrowed artery, it causes heart attack or stroke. Numerous studies have concluded that garlic significantly lowers LDL (bad) cholesterol; others have concluded it does not. One study found that aged garlic extract protected LDL against oxidation by free radicals. A study using raw garlic found no such effect. A comparison of garlic eaters and garlic abstainers in India found that the garlic eaters had significantly lower levels of LDL, triglycerides, and body fats.

Garlic's cholesterol-lowering reputation took a nosedive when a Stanford University study claimed to "drive a stake through claims that garlic lowers cholesterol." The widely publicized study helmed by nutrition researcher Christopher Gardner concluded that neither eating raw garlic nor taking garlic supplements lowers LDL cholesterol in people with moderately elevated cholesterol levels, meaning those people most likely to eat garlic or take supplements to reduce their cholesterol. While lab tests had shown that allicin inhibits the synthesis of cholesterol, some question remained about whether it would react the same way inside the human body. As Gardner said, "In lab tests, you can apply the garlic compounds directly to cells, but in real people you don't know whether allicin would actually get directly to cells if someone ate garlic." While the participants in the Stanford study didn't lower their cholesterol, they did get to eat 30,000 gourmet sandwiches that were created and taste-tested just for them.

Immunity and Antioxidant Properties

In addition to boosting the immune system by killing bacterial, fungal, and viral infections, garlic stimulates the activity of macrophages, natural killer (NK) cells, and T-helper cells. Macrophages (from the Greek for "big eaters") are cells that protect the body by engulfing and

Stanford Study Sandwiches

Stanford is in Menlo Park, just up the road from Gilroy, California. At the beginning of the study, Gardner drove to Gilroy to buy eight cases of fresh garlic. When he brought them back, an eight-person team from Stanford Dining Services spent two weeks peeling and mashing the garlic with a pestle. The team then had to determine how to "deliver" the garlic to the study participants surmising, correctly I think, that it would be a bit much to ask people to eat a frozen tablet of mashed garlic six days a week for six months. They decided to come up with delicious sandwiches to encourage people to participate in the study. Twelve recipes were developed and taste-tested before six sandwiches were selected for the study. Participants (aka lucky bastards) came to Stanford twice a week to pick up three sandwiches. They'd eat one that day, one the next, and one the day after so the garlic had to be active and fresh three days after they picked up the sandwiches.

The team also realized that they had to provide sandwiches not only to the fresh garlic group, but also to the other partici-pants so that if the fresh garlic group reported lower cholesterol, there could be no possibility that the sandwiches, all of which were designed to be heart healthy, had been responsible. So par-ticipants in the garlic pill and placebo groups also got sandwiches, but without the garlic. Gardner's favorite? Portobello mushroom on focaccia.

devouring harmful foreign particles including viruses, bacteria, and yeast. Macrophages may also stimulate other immune cells including NK cells, which provide rapid responses to virally infected cells and respond to tumor formation. T-helper cells, as the name suggests, as-sist other white blood cells in performing their immunity-boosting activities.

Garlic is also a good source of antioxidants, which protect your cells from damaging free radicals. Free radicals are rapacious atoms with an unpaired electron that's desperate to pair with another molecule. In their quest to bond, free radicals attack other molecules to steal an electron and become stable. In so doing, they create a new free radical. This theft of electrons creates a chain reaction of free radicals that may attack, damage, and kill healthy cells. Free radicals are linked to aging, tissue damage, arthritis, diabetes, heart disease, and some kinds of cancer. They may also play a role in neurodegenerative diseases like Parkinson's and Alzheimer's. Antioxidants are molecules that can safely interact with free radicals and stop the chain reaction before it damages healthy cells. Garlic's role as an antioxidant comes from its organosulfuric compounds, as well as its vitamin C and selenium. Selenium is an essential trace mineral that the body cannot manufacture, so it needs to be supplied by diet.

Garlic's selenium and sulfur also stimulate the production of glutathione, a powerful antioxidant that breaks down toxins, protects and repairs cell membranes and DNA, and helps in the removal and detoxification of carcinogens. A deficiency of glutathione is found in patients suffering from heart disease, liver disease, cancer, diabetes, Alzheimer's, Parkinson's, asthma, autism, and arthritis.

Garlic grows well in selenium-rich soil and can absorb large quantities of selenium without being poisoned. While a large garlic clove provides less than 2 percent of a person's daily value (DV) of selenium, a clove of selenium-enriched garlic can provide four times a person's required allowance.

Pregnancy and Fetal Health

Pregnant woman needn't avoid and probably should eat garlic during their pregnancies. Some studies have suggested that garlic may help to lower the risk of pre-eclampsia, a potentially dangerous condition that causes high blood pressure, and may also help increase, in utero, the birth weight of underweight babies. Also, a study by bio-psychologists Julie

Mennella and Gary Beauchamp showed that nursing infants like the flavor of garlic and will eat more when their mother's milk is infused with it.

Cancer Prevention

It's not often that you see "cancer" and "good news" together, but the National Cancer Institute, part of the National Institutes of Health, recognizes garlic as one of several vegetables with potentially powerful anticancer properties.

Scientists today believe that eating garlic can reduce the risk of several cancers, especially those of the gastrointestinal tract (stomach, colon, rectum, and esophagus), and may lower the risk of getting cancers of the breast, prostate, liver, and pancreas. To fully recognize and realize garlic's cancer-fighting potential, however, scientists have a lot more work to do.

In addition to its antioxidant properties, garlic's cancer-fighting potential can be attributed to its allyl sulfur compounds and their ability to block the formation of carcinogenic nitrosamines as well as boost garlic's powerful antiviral activities. Allyl sulfur compounds may prevent the transformation of normal cells to tumorous cells, may delay or inhibit the onset of cancer, help the body both flush out carcinogens, and cause cancer cells to die naturally.

PhIP, another carcinogenic chemical formed when meat, poultry, and fish are cooked at high temperatures, has been linked to breast cancer, and studies have shown that women who eat large quantities of meat have higher incidences of breast cancer. Diallyl disulfide, a garlic-derived compound, has been found to inhibit the effects of PiHP and may play a significant role in preventing breast cancer.

Scientists estimate that roughly 15 percent of all human cancers can be attributed to viruses. Research indicates that garlic may help to both prevent and inhibit the cancer-causing viruses hepatitis (liver cancer) and human papilloma (cervical cancer).

Helicobacter pylori bacteria have been implicaated in stomach cancer, and a number of new studies suggest that H. pylori may also be a contributing factor in pancreatic cancer. Pancreatic cancer has a 96 percent mortality rate and is one of the worst kinds of cancer you can get because it's not usually diagnosed (or diagnosable) until it's too late to treat. These same studies also indict Porphyrmomonas gingivalis (an oral bacteria usually associated with periodontal disease) as a possible cause of pancreatic cancer. In addition to its potential action against H. pylori, garlic is effective in both inhibiting and killing P. gingivalis, so it may help to reduce the incidence of this horrific disease. A study conducted in the San Francisco Bay area found that pancreatic cancer risk was 54 percent lower in people who ate large amounts of garlic. (My father died of pancreatic cancer so I'm especially attuned to its insidiousness.)

Scientists at the Medical University of South Carolina recently found that garlic was found effective against another death sentence, glioblastoma, an aggressive type of brain tumor with a survival rate of less than one year. Although the test was in the lab and the results require further study, this was the first direct evidence that the garlic-derived compound diallyl disulfide is effective in blocking pathways of the proliferation of cancer cells and ultimately may help reduce tumor growth in patients with this most lethal brain tumor.

Anti-Inflammatory

Garlic's anti-inflammatory properties come from sulfuric compounds that help relieve symptoms of some auto-immune diseases like rheumatoid arthritis, as well as symptoms of asthma, psoriasis, allergies, and cold sores. Garlic may even help to prevent weight gain and assist in weight loss (which is amazing news). Researchers increasingly believe that obesity is a low-grade inflammatory disease and that inflammation converts pre-fat cells into fat cells. Garlic's anti-inflammatory properties may be able to inhibit this process, thus stopping pre-fat cells from becoming fat cells. While garlic may also relieve symptoms from diseases caused by gastrointestinal inflammation (ulcerative colitis, Crohn's, and irritable bowel syndrome) in some sufferers, it triggers outbreaks in others.

Heavy Metal Toxicity

Heavy metal poisoning, the accumulation of toxic levels of various metals in the human body, is another growing threat to modern society as poisoning from lead, mercury, arsenic, cadmium, and copper approaches epidemic proportions. Humans are exposed to heavy metals in hazardous waste sites and industrial settings as well as in our food, water, homes, pesticides, and medicines.

The human body is unable to metabolize high levels of these metals and when toxic levels are reached, they accumulate in the body's soft tissues and cause a range of symptoms from fatigue and memory loss to irreversible neurological damage and organ damage. Prolonged exposure may cause cancer or produce degenerative symptoms similar to those of Parkinson's disease, Alzheimer's disease, muscular dystrophy, and multiple sclerosis.

Studies have shown that thanks to its sulfuric compounds, garlic can detoxify heavy metals in the body and is also a natural chelation agent. (*Chelation* comes from the Greek word for "claw," and it's a process by which an organic compound, in this case sulfur, bonds with metal.) Chelation therapy is the process of drawing toxic substances out of the body's cells and into the bloodstream so they can be eliminated.

Several years ago, scientists from the World Health Organization found that the groundwater in Bangladesh was contaminated by naturally occurring arsenic and that between 35 and 77 million of the country's 125 million inhabitants were affected by arsenic. Studies in India demonstrated that the sulfur-containing substances in garlic "scavenged arsenic from tissues and blood." One of the study's authors, Keya Chaudhuri of the Indian Institute of Chemical Biology, advised people in areas at risk for arsenic poisoning to eat one to three cloves of garlic per day as a preventative.

Another recent study in India even found that waste from the processing and canning of garlic and onions could be used to remove heavy metals from contaminated industrial materials, in effect, using garlic and onions to stem the problem of heavy metal toxicity at its source.

This affordable and environmentally friendly technology could be a boon for companies in developing countries.

Men's Health

Garlic has been appreciated for its aphrodisiacal properties for centuries, primarily due to its ability to improve blood circulation. It may be especially helpful to men with heart disease who may suffer from impotence due to poor circulation and hardening of the arteries in the groin area. As garlic addresses both of these conditions, it may be a potent natural cure for erectile dysfunction. In 2007, the BBC broadcast research results issued by Coldiretti, an Italian farming trade union, which claimed that eating four cloves of garlic a day for three months was as good as Viagra. True or not, it will shock no one that garlic sales in Great Britain jumped by 32 percent.

Garlic also stimulates the production of nitric oxide synthase, the enzyme that is required for men to obtain an erection and may help to promote prostate health. Research suggests that garlic may reduce prostate mass, increase urine flow, and decrease urinary frequency in men with benign prostatic hyperplasia (enlarged prostate). Studies in both China and the United States found that men who ate more than ten grams of alliums (especially garlic and scallions) reduced their risk of getting prostate cancer by 50 percent. And in men who have prostate cancer, promising results from a small study suggest that garlic may significantly lower prostate-specific antigen (PSA) levels, which are often, though not always, an indication of prostate cancer. While much of this research is in its early stages, as in other areas of study, initial results certainly warrant additional investigation.

Conclusion

With all this potential, it should not be shocking that the World Health Organization recommends daily consumption of garlic in its guidelines for general health. And that's welcome news when so much of what we're taught to do to live a long, healthy life is tiring (exercise six times a week for at least thirty minutes) or just plain annoying (eat chocolate chip cookies in moderation). So isn't it nice to hear, "Eat some garlic. It's good for you."

⌁ Dr. Garlic

South Africa's former health minister, Manto Tshabalala-Msimang, drew international condemnation for refusing to acknowledge the link between HIV and AIDS. She recommended that AIDS patients consume olive oil, the African potato, beets, lemon, and garlic instead of the newly available antiretroviral drugs. Her policy was responsible for thousands of premature deaths and earned her the nickname Dr. Garlic. Tshabalala-Msimang said, "Raw garlic and a skin of the lemon—not only do they give you a beautiful face and skin but they also protect you from disease."

In 2004, Fana Khaba, a well-known Johannesburg radio talk show host and DJ, also shunned the drugs in favor of a juice fast made of lemon, olive oil, beets, and garlic that he called "Africa's Solution." Khaba continued to tout the benefits of his diet as AIDS ravaged his body. He died the same year.

Caveats

Here are a few cautionary words on the use and consumption of garlic.

Because of its high sulfuric content, garlic can burn the skin, so don't leave a garlic compress on for a prolonged period of time or overnight. It may inhibit blood clotting, so patients are advised to stop eating a lot of garlic or taking garlic supplements seven days before surgery and people taking aspirin or warfarin to thin the blood should also consult with their doctor before consuming any form of garlic.

Garlic may exaggerate the activity of medications that inhibit the action of platelets in the body. Garlic may significantly reduce the blood serum levels of protease inhibitors, a class of antiretroviral drugs used to treat people with HIV/AIDS and hepatitis.

Garlic may reduce the effectiveness of isoniazid (an anti-tubercular medication), cyclosporine (which prevents organ rejection in transplant patients), and birth control pills. It may also increase the risk of bleeding when taken with NSAIDs. And although evidence is scant, garlic may amplify the effect of diabetes medications taken to lower blood sugar, which may in turn lead to hypoglycemia, a large drop in the level of sugar in the blood that can be fatal.

two

LIBERTÉ, EGALITÉ, GARLIC SOUFFLÉ: GARLIC AND FOOD

"Tomatoes and oregano make it Italian. Wine and tarragon make it French. Sour cream makes it Russian. Lemon and cinnamon make it Greek. Soy sauce makes it Chinese. Garlic makes it good."

—Alice May Brock, author of *Alice's Restaurant Cookbook*

Preserved garlic cloves and remnants found in ancient caves and tombs strongly suggest that our ancestors have been using garlic as a food seasoning since their hunting and gathering days. Some speculate that humans may have started using garlic 10,000 years ago, just after the last Ice Age. Garlic was domesticated during the Neolithic period when humans evolved from seminomadic hunter-gatherers to sedentary farmers. This seismic agricultural transition completely changed the way people lived. They built permanent dwellings and started communities that evolved into modern cities. They started growing food on farms, trading goods, and learning to cultivate crops and domesticate animals. This in turn gave rise to the great ancient civilizations (and cuisines) of Egypt, Greece, Rome, Mesopotamia, China, and India. These civilizations found endless ways to whet their appetite for this robust, celebrated, infamous food.

AN ANCIENT DELICACY

The evolution of cities created a financial opportunity for merchants who ferried goods on the routes between Asia and Europe. Since garlic is lightweight, long-storing, a good source of energy and nutrients, and powerful enough to cover up the taste of spoiled food, it was the perfect accompaniment for long, arduous journeys. Garlic was included on a list of dietary staples that a scribe carved into a clay tablet in 2600 B.C.E. and was an ingredient in three of the world's oldest known recipes. These Sumerian recipes, which one hopes tasted better than they sound, were a goat stew with fat, garlic, onions, sour milk, and blood; bird stew with garlic, onions, malt cake, and milk; and braised turnips with fat, cumin, coriander, leeks, and garlic.

Egyptian rulers fed garlic to their slaves, and it gave strength to the builders of the Great Pyramids of Giza around 2560 B.C.E. Pyramid inscriptions document that workers ate garlic, radishes, and onions valued at 1,600 talents of silver—over $30 million in today's currency. Garlic was also at the root of the world's first recorded labor strike. During a garlic shortage, slaves refused to work when their masters reduced and then eliminated their daily ration. (Can you blame them?) Once the garlic ration was reinstated, construction on the pyramids resumed. At the time, garlic was considered so valuable that fifteen pounds of it were sufficient to purchase one healthy, male slave.

The competitors in the first Olympic Games, held in 776 B.C.E., also ate garlic to increase their stamina, making it nature's first recorded performance-enhancing drug (and a legal one at that). The first thirteen Olympiads were more like an Olympic Game as there was only one competition: a 200-yard foot race. Competitors trained rigorously for ten months and realized the importance of nutritious food in their diet so perhaps it's not surprising that the first Olympic champion was named Koroibos, a cook.

Both the Olympics (in which only men competed) and its sister games, the Heraia, a sporting competition among unmarried women, were dominated by the famously vigorous (and unsentimental) men and women of Sparta. (To test the hardiness of their constitutions, Spartan newborns were bathed in wine instead of water; those deemed unfit for future military service were abandoned or thrown into a chasm.) Unlike elsewhere in ancient Greece, Spartan women were taught to be independent and physically active, competing in wrestling, javelin and discus throwing, and foot and horse races. As all citizens of Sparta ate the same thing (by legal decree), we can assume that, like the men, the women fueled themselves with garlic before their competitions. Consistent with their fierce athletic prowess, the men of Sparta were once the world's most feared military force. They ate garlic to boost their legendary strength as well as to heal wounds suffered in battle. Soldiers from other Greek city-states also fueled themselves with garlic for battle as Aristophanes illustrates in his comic play, *The Acharnians.* He wrote of aroused Thracian soldiers "all dosed up with garlic," an allusion to the ancient Greek fondness for cock fighting in which competitors would feed their birds garlic and rub it on their bodies believing it made them more aggressive. (Aristophanes's obscene association of garlic-aroused soldiers and garlic-primed cocks was not coincidental.)

As Marcus Aurelius illustrated, upper-class Romans detested garlic's strong odor with one notable exception—Julius Caesar, who was said to consume garlic with gusto but had no hand in the creation of his eponymous salad. Garlic is associated with the planet Mars, which was named after the Roman god of war, so it seems fitting that Roman generals gave their soldiers garlic to inspire them and give them courage. The soldiers also planted garlic in the fields of the countries they conquered in the belief that garlic-inspired courage could be transmitted up through the battlefield. Thanks to this practice, the Roman legions deserve credit for introducing garlic to the countries of northern Europe. There was even a saying at the time, *Allia non comedas* (May you not eat garlic), which really meant, "May you not be drafted into the army."

Garlic was also considered suitable for lowly peasants, and the poet

Virgil even wrote a poem about a peasant who sets about to collect ingredients and prepare his evening meal. The poem is called "Moretum" after the garlic cheese spread he makes. (For a modern recipe for moretum, see page 244.) For reasons unfathomable to me, moretum was an appealing subject for writers of both poetry and prose in ancient Rome. Scholars have speculated that the Roman lyric poet Horace was served moretum when he dined with his friend and patron Maecenas, although it is unlikely that such a rustic dish would have been served at the table of a well-known patron of the arts. Whatever garlicky dish he ate, Horace hated it and declared, "If e'er a parricide with hand accursed hath cut a father's venerable throat, Hemlock's too mild a poison—give him garlic." Horace's "Epode 3" describes the poet's garlic-induced indigestion and is probably the most eloquent takedown of garlic ever published. In addition to citing garlic's use by Medea, Horace compares it to the blood of a viper, the fiery vapors of Sirius the Dog-Star, and the poison that caused the death of Hercules, as well as suggesting that his dinner might have been tampered with by the child-killing demon-witch Canidia. Cursing Maecenas with sexual rejection on account of his bad breath, the good-natured poet jokingly says to him, "I hope your girlfriend fights back your kisses and gives you a wide berth in bed."

Whatever he served, Maecenas (or more likely, his servant) did not get the recipe from *De re coquinaria,* the only known cookbook of ancient Roman recipes, and therefore, the only insight we have into the dining habits of the time. Since it was intended for the upper class, no one (but Horace) will be surprised to learn that there isn't so much as a whiff of garlic in a single recipe.

NOMADS ON THE SILK ROAD

The Silk Road was not a one-way street, so while some merchants, traders, and nomads were ferrying garlic and other goods westward toward Europe, others were traveling east and south to the uncharted frontiers of China, India, Korea, and beyond. Garlic's northeastern journey from

Central Asia took it across the majestic mountains, high desert plateaus, and deep fertile basins of the sparsely populated regions of Tibet, Xinjiang, and Mongolia en route to the banks of the Yellow River, the cradle of Chinese civilization. (It's believed that nomads introduced garlic to Mesopotamia, China, and India at about the same time.)

The Chinese character for garlic is one symbol, which indicates that it's one of the language's first written words. In the *Shih ching* (*Book of Odes*), the earliest known collection of Chinese poems, hymns, and songs, one poem tells of nomadic herders who were roasting spring lamb with garlic over the fire. As the smell rises, God asks, "What smell is this, so strong and good?" Mindful of this, sacrificial lambs were seasoned with garlic to make them more appealing to the gods.

The link between food and medicine in China dates back to Huang-ti's *The Yellow Emperor's Classic of Medicine* and has remained unbroken, so it's not surprising that garlic plays a starring role in the cuisine of many provinces of China. Huang-ti realized that if he was to be a great ruler, he must first be able to govern himself, and this included using food as medicine to prolong his life. The cuisine of subsequent imperial courts also featured medicinal foods to extend the life span and quality of life of the ruler and his court. Beginning in 1115 B.C.E., the imperial court appointed a dietician to both supervise the cooking and track the physical and mental effects that the meals had on the emperor. Some of the craftsmanship was so intricate that some chefs spent their entire lives perfecting one dish.

Huang-ti relied on the ancient concept of yin and yang, the balance of opposite but complementary colors, flavors, and textures. Yin foods have cooling properties while yang foods are warming. Eating too much of one kind of food is believed to throw a body off-balance both physically and spiritually. Garlic is a yang food, which helps to explain its popularity in the colder climates of northern China. (Garlic is also used in many of the celebrated cuisines of southern China but the taste tends to be subtler.) Those yang properties help to explain why garlic accents vegetables so well, as all vegetables except seaweed are yin.

Of the eight, great regional culinary schools of China, which evolved from ancient times, four (Cantonese, Hunan, Shandong, and Sichuan) are heavily laced with garlic. Cantonese cuisine is known for its light, fresh, unspicy taste though garlic is used as a seasoning extensively and sometimes exclusively. The cuisines of Hunan and Sichuan are both hot and spicy, but differ in that the fiery sauces of Hunan get their heat from red chilies and garlic, which are used fresh, in infused oils, and in spice pastes. Sichuan cooks, not surprisingly, use the Sichuan peppercorn for spiciness and augment it with garlic, ginger, and fermented soybeans. The cuisine centered in northern China originated in the garlic-growing province of Shandong (and strongly influenced the cuisine of Beijing). Shandong cuisine is noted for its combination of pungent flavors including garlic, ginger, and leeks. Although Fujian cuisine doesn't use much garlic in its preparations, it's used extensively in dipping sauces and in the condiment Shacha, a pungent oil spiced with garlic, shallots, chilies, and dried shrimp. (The other three culinary schools, Anhui, Jiangsu, and Zhejiang, use garlic sparingly if at all.)

Garlic is also prevalent in some of China's lesser-known provinces. When Marco Polo traveled across China in the thirteenth century, he was astounded to find that the villagers in the southern province of Yunnan ate the raw flesh of fowl, sheep, oxen, and buffalo in "garlic sauce mixed with good spice." The taste for raw meat persists in southwest China and special occasions there call for one or more freshly slaughtered raw pigs, finely minced and served with a garlic-chili-soy sauce. In the cold, northern province of Heilongjiang, which borders Inner Mongolia and Russia, people eat lots of Russian foods. In the early twentieth century, Russian traders brought garlic and black pepper–spiced smoked pork sausage across the border. Today, Harbin Red Sausage is the city's specialty while in the northern province of Jilin, which borders North Korea, residents share the Korean love of pickled vegetables as well as dog meat topped with garlic.

Korea's prodigious garlic consumption is linked to their love of kimchi—the garlicky, peppery, pickled cabbage dish that they've been fermenting for centuries. Kimchi is widely regarded as Korea's national food and symbol. There's even a saying that "the taste of kimchi is the taste of your mother's fingertips." Like the Jews, the Koreans are also derisively referred to as garlic eaters, primarily by the garlic-averse Japanese.

In addition to introducing garlic to the Japanese as a medicine, the Chinese and the Koreans exported Buddhism and its garlic-averse vegetarian cuisine to Japan. Japan's Zen Buddhist cuisine is called Shojin Ryori: *shojin* means asceticism in pursuit of enlightenment; *ryori* means cooking. This temple cuisine, eaten by Buddhist monks, considers garlic one of five pungent vegetables known as *gokun* that are believed to stress the five visceral organs (stomach, intestines, liver, spleen, and pancreas) and as such, it is prohibited.

There is one Japanese area that has a long history of eating garlic and that's the prefecture of Kochi on the southern coast of the island of Shikoko. Kochi's signature dish is Katsuo-No-Tataki, a lightly-grilled bonito fish topped with lots of raw garlic, ginger, and green onions. The prevalence of garlic eaters in Kochi for thousands of years is most likely due to the domination of the Chosokabe clan, which had ancestral roots in Korea. (The people of Kochi are notoriously strong willed; the women are called *Hachikin,* which means "eight balls," as they are said to be able to hold their liquor better than four men.)

To reach the subcontinent of India, garlic traveled along the rugged mountain paths south from the Tien Shan mountains through the Pamir Mountains (known as the "onion" mountains in Chinese thanks to the wild onions that grow at its high altitude). Garlic arrived in the Indus Valley, home to a vast and advanced Bronze Age civilization that inhabited what is now Pakistan and western India, as well as parts of Iran and Afghanistan. While food is essential for all human life, there is probably no culture that recognizes the importance of food more than that of India. In ancient texts, food is regarded as the source of all life and called *Brahma* (Lord of All Creatures).

Searching a settlement that thrived 4,500 years ago, archaeologists found a carbonized clove of garlic alongside remnants of ginger and turmeric suggesting that Indians have been enjoying highly spiced curry dishes for thousands of years, long before the Arab, Chinese, and European traders imported spices from southeast Asia.

In Ayurveda, garlic is believed to be one of the few things that possesses five of the six *rasas* (or tastes) and for that reason is called *rason* (king of the rasas). Garlic's five rasas are sweet, salty, pungent, bitter, and astringent; it does not have the rasa for sour. As Ayurveda advocates a diet that includes all six rasas, garlic would seem to be an almost perfect food. Alas, food is precisely where the plot thickens. In Ayurveda, foods are grouped into three categories—sattvic, rajasic, and tamasic—which promote, respectively, goodness, passion, and ignorance. Garlic is rajasic and tamasic, meaning it promotes passion (and its handmaidens, aggravation, anxiety, and aggression) as well as ignorance.

Although garlic as a food is suspect within certain circles, throughout the subcontinent, taste clearly trumps medicine and religion. Indian food is unimaginable without garlic and although India is the world's second-largest producer of garlic, it's so essential to the native cuisine that additional garlic has to be imported to satisfy demand. Garlic, ginger, and onions are the Holy Trinity of Indian cooking. Garlic and ginger are generally used in equal quantities because it's believed that ginger raises blood pressure and garlic lowers it, so together they keep diners in balance.

India is the world's original melting pot with many of its most celebrated dishes influenced by invaders from Central Asia, Arabia, Persia, Portugal, and Britain. Muslim incursions in northern India produced the rich, creamy Mughlai cuisine that's served in most Indian restaurants in the United States. This Persian-influenced aromatic cuisine features garlic and ginger pastes augmented by a wide array of spices, dried fruits, and nuts. The cuisine of Goa, on India's southwestern coast, is a melding of native Konkan recipes with the aromatic influence of the spice-loving Portuguese who had ruled over the state for centuries. The region is known for its searingly hot vindaloos, a marinade of vinegar, chilies, and garlic in which meats are stewed. The word *vindaloo* is a combination of *vin* (vinegar) and *aloo* from *alho*, the Portuguese word for "garlic."

In the eastern state of West Bengal and its capital Calcutta, garlic and ginger are enhanced with mustard oil, as essential to Bengali cuisine as olive oil is to the cuisine of the Mediterranean. While much of the cuisine of Gujarat in western India is influenced by its garlic- and onion-averse Buddhist and Jain inhabitants, the region is also known for a pungent condiment made from garlic, salt, and an abundance of dried red chilies. Thus while garlic is shunned by some Indian religions, it plays a vital role in the country's remarkably diverse cuisines.

⌁ Gandhi and Garlic

Mahatma Gandhi had very high blood pressure and his doctors recommended garlic as a remedy. A medical doctor who was consulted on his treatment wrote that Gandhi, though "inconveniently inquisitive at the beginning . . . was the most enthusiastic follower of a principle once he was convinced about its soundness." Later, author and Gandhi biographer Ved Mehta recalled that Gandhi "always had a big bowl of crushed garlic by his plate" and that "he ate a lot of it and dished some out to anyone who he had decided needed it."

The golden age of Islam extended to cuisine and reached its pinnacle in the medieval cooking of ninth-century Baghdad, which was the richest city in the world at the time. Fortunately for us, an Arab scribe documented the Persian-inspired dishes served to aristocrats in *Kitab al-tabikh* (*The Book of Cookery*). Hummus and falafel were nowhere to be found here, but garlic was. Garlic, yogurt, and mint were a popular marinade for kebabs. As Persian cooking used large quantities of spices, blending both sweet and savory ingredients, a typical sauce might include garlic, tahini, lemon juice, and cinnamon. The traditional herbs used in contemporary Arab cooking—mint, parsley, and cilantro—were augmented with basil, tarragon, rue, caraway, asafetida, saffron, and ginger in addition to nonherbal ingredients like pomegranates, dates, dried fruits, nuts, vinegar, rose petals, and of course, garlic. The armies of the Crusades went on to introduce many of these exotic ingredients to Europe.

Garlic made it as far as Scandinavia where it had a brief moment in the northern sun during the Dark Ages when Vikings loaded garlic on their ships to flavor their food and protect themselves from illness and evil spirits during long journeys. With the demise of the Viking Age in 1050 C.E., garlic's popularity in Scandinavia plummeted and little is found in the indigenous cuisines of the region.

FLOURISHING IN EUROPE

Thanks to the monks' cultivation of garlic in medieval Europe, it became widely available and inexpensive, which was especially welcome in times when living conditions were wildly unsanitary and refrigeration was but a dream. Society was highly stratified and food consumption differed widely between the classes. However, it appears that garlic was one of the few things eaten across classes. Elaborate banquets were the primary leisure pursuit of royals and nobles who feasted on dishes seasoned with exotic spices and seasonings that were far too expensive for members of the working class. Our garlic-cultivating monks and other clergy also ate a high-class diet thanks to the bounty growing within the grounds of the monasteries. Many monks came from aristocratic families and no oath of poverty was going to stand in the way of a good meal. Philippa Patrick of the Institute of Archaeology at University College, London, analyzed the skeletons from three monastic burial sites in England and concluded that medieval monks were extremely overweight thanks to an average daily consumption of roughly six thousand calories. The monks raised animals to supply butter, eggs, milk, and cheese and ate the animals once they had outlived their usefulness. Monasteries were filled with extensive gardens and fish ponds. The monks' intake of vegetables was limited to beans, peas, onions, leeks, and garlic.

Perhaps no European country is more closely identified with garlic than France, where one could argue that the pungent bulb reached its culinary and cultural apogee. Former premier Paul Reynaud explained that the body of a Frenchman is composed not of the scientific elements that make up other mortals, but rather "a simple compound of pepper, garlic, pâté de foie gras, common bread, and good red wine of the land."

Garlic has long been far more popular in the south of France than in the north where onions take pride of place. The earliest known mention of garlic in a French cookbook was in 1306, where it is one of only five herbs and vegetables used. In his *Grand Dictionnaire de Cuisine,* Alexandre Dumas summed up the pervasiveness of garlic in Provence when he wrote that the air is "impregnated with the aroma of garlic, which makes it very healthful to breathe." Covering all bases, he also wrote, "Everybody knows the odor of garlic except the one who has eaten it and wonders why everybody turns away from him."

Guillaume Tirel, known as Taillevent, was the cook to the Court of France in the mid-fourteenth century. His cookbook, *Le viandier,* provided the foundation for French gastronomy. His book includes green and white garlic sauces as well as a sauce of garlic steeped in grape must that was served with herring. He also included a recipe for cameline sauce with garlic. Cameline sauce (sweet spices, bread, and garlic steeped in vinegar) was a very popular sauce in medieval times and could even be purchased ready-made at local markets.

The glorious aroma of Provence can be credited to the region's most famous specialties (and culprits): bouillabaisse, the legendary garlic-topped seafood melange; and aioli, which gets its name from the French words for garlic and oil. Aioli so captures the essence of Provence, that Nobel Prize–winning poet Frédéric Mistral called his Provençal journal *L'Aiòli.* As Peter Mayle observed in *Provence A–Z,* the lyrical Mistral was nothing if not practical. In 1891, he observed, "Aioli epitomizes the heat, the power, and the joy of the Provençal sun, but it has another virtue—it drives away flies." Mayle also wrote about an annual Provençal event, the *aioli monstre* (grand aioli), when villagers welcome summer with a colorful feast of fresh vegetables, poached fish, and meats, all of which are dipped into and poured over with the rich, garlicky mayonnaise.

The aroma of garlic is so strongly associated with the French that during WWII, Charles Fraser-Smith (the inspiration for James Bond's gadget guru Q) created garlic-flavored chocolate tablets for agents parachuting into France so that their breath smelled suitably Gallic.

The French passion for garlic is well known and well documented; the English attitude toward garlic, however, is less predictable and more mercurial. While it's widely assumed that the British upper class eschewed garlic during medieval times, a peek at recipes from two of Britain's oldest cookbooks suggests otherwise. In April 2013, Faith Wallis, a professor of medieval studies at McGill University, was reading through a twelfth-century manuscript from the monastery at Durham when she came upon a collection of recipes that she realized predated the previous earliest known British recipe collection by 150 years. The recipes, which were used by monks to entertain members of the aristocracy, included "hen in winter" (chicken with garlic, pepper, and sage), and the sauces typically featured parsley, sage, pepper, mustard, coriander, and (you guessed it) garlic!

Until this recent discovery, *The Forme of Cury* was considered Britain's oldest cookbook. Published in 1395, *The Forme of Cury* is a collection of highly spiced recipes written by the master-chefs of King Richard II. (*Cury* comes not from curry, but from the Latin *curare*, which means both to dress foods and to cure illness, reinforcing the connection between food and medicine.) Garlic is included, raw, in a salad of twelve herbs and vegetables; with grapes in a dressing for roast goose; boiled in water and oil; and sprinkled with saffron, salt, and strong spices as a side dish.

Looking at garlic's role in *The Canterbury Tales*, written at the end of the fourteenth century, it's easy to understand why we thought garlic was relegated to commoners. Chaucer conveyed the baseness of the low-class Summoner by mentioning, "Well loved he garleek, oynons, and eek lekes, / And for to drinken strong wyn, reed as blood." Roughly two centuries later, Shakespeare expressed the same disdain.

Shakespeare mentions garlic in five of his plays where it is used exclusively as an insult and a mark of low class. In *A Midsummer Night's Dream*, Bottom extols his fellow actors in the play within the play, to "eat no onions nor garlic, for we are to utter sweet breath." Hotspur issues a scathing insult in *Henry IV, Part 1,* when he declared, "I had rather live with cheese and garlic in a windmill, far, than feed on cates [delicacies] and have him talk to me in any summerhouse in Christendom." Lucio talks of the Duke, who would "mouth with a beggar, though she smelt brown bread and garlic" in *Measure for Measure.* In *Coriolanus,* Menenius rebukes the tribunes for their foolishness in hanging on the "breath of garlic-eaters" over that of noble Coriolanus. And in *The Winter's Tale,* Dorcas gives garlic to Mopsa, her rival for Clown's attention, saying, "Mopsa must be your mistress: marry, garlic to mend her kissing with!" implying that garlic would improve her rival's breath. Some of the Elizabethan audiences at Shakespeare's plays could be similarly indicted for garlic breath. The groundlings, those who paid one cent to stand in the pit area of the theater, were known to chomp on garlic cloves, causing the upper-class patrons in the balconies above to refer to them as "penny stinkards." (Shakespeare's fellow dramatist Thomas Dekker concurred, calling the groundlings "garlic-mouthed stinkers.")

Cervantes's views of garlic echo those of his Elizabethan contemporary, Shakespeare. In *Don Quixote,* Cervantes's protagonist cautions his squire, Sancho Panza, "Do not eat garlic or onions; for their smell will reveal that you are a peasant." Later, as his beloved Dulcinea approaches, Quixote decries, "I got such a sniff of raw garlic as stank me out and poisoned me to the heart." Sancho, seeking to placate his distressed master, convinces him that evil magicians have stolen Dulcinea's lovely scent and replaced it with garlic, transforming her into a common peasant girl.

The "dainty" English upper crust also used garlic to disparage the Italians, who have also been saddled with the sobriquet "garlic eaters." The Italian affection for garlic goes back to ancient Rome, and the smell of garlic has been associated with them ever since. British writer Horace Walpole referred to Italians as the "rascally garlic tribe" and poet Percy Bysshe Shelley, writing in 1818 of his travels in Italy, asked, "What do you think? Young women of rank eat—you will never guess what—garlick!"

John Evelyn, who published the first English-language book of salads in 1699, would concur. In *John Evelyn's Acetaria: A Discourse of Sallets,* garlic was strictly forbidden "by reason of its intolerable rankness."

He considered garlic fit only for "rustic northerns . . . or such as use the sea." Evelyn doesn't stop there but goes on to declare it "part of the Punishment of such as had committed the horrid'st Crimes," before concluding, "To be sure, 'tis not for Ladies Palats, nor those who court them."

⌒ The Columbian Exchange

Columbus's arrival in Hispaniola heralded the beginning of the Columbian Exchange, the trade of goods between the Old World and the New World. In addition to garlic, the New World received cattle, pigs, wheat, chickens, sheep, donkeys, rice, oats, barley, rye, onions, lettuce, cabbage, and bananas—none of which were indigenous to the region. And among the items the Old World received in return were llamas, potatoes, tomatoes, bell peppers, and chilies.

The classic Spanish cold soup, gazpacho, owes its modern incarnation to the Columbian Exchange. Gazpacho was originally made from stale bread, garlic, olive oil, salt, and vinegar. When tomatoes and bell peppers were brought to Europe, they were added to gazpacho and have become traditional recipe ingredients. While the explorers brought the initial shipments, colonists and missionaries are credited with spreading the Old World foods, including garlic, to the southern states of America and throughout Central and South America.

The Russians have long been garlic eaters, and some say that garlic is the Russians' third doctor. (The *banya*, or bathhouse, being the first, and vodka, the second). This was documented by two seventeenth-century travelers. Sir Thomas Smith, an English visitor to Russia wrote of the cuisine, "Garlick and onions must be-sauce many of my words as they did the most part of their dishes." Adam Olearius, a German scholar and (highly undiplomatic) diplomat concurred. Of his visits with the Russians, he wrote, "They generally prepare their food with garlic and onion so all the rooms and houses, including the sumptuous chambers of the Grand Prince's palace in the Kremlin, give off an odor offensive to us Germans." It gets worse. He goes on to say, "After a meal, they do not refrain in the presence and hearing of all, from releasing what nature produces, fore and aft. Since they eat a great deal of garlic and onions, it's trying to be in their presence." One of his fellow travelers even composed a little ditty: "Churches, icons, crosses, bells. Painted whores and garlic smells. Vice and vodka every place. This is Moscow's daily face." Or, as a friend of mine said, "My kind of town."

Garlic was so valuable in Russia that in Siberia in the seventeenth and eighteenth century, you could use it to pay your taxes. The tax rate was fifteen bulbs for a man, ten bulbs for a woman, and five for a child. Resist the temptation to try this with the IRS.

While garlic was slow to catch on in the United States, it did have a brief reprieve in the late eighteenth and early nineteenth century when upper-class kitchens embraced exotic ingredients and complex cooking methods. First Lady Martha Washington had recipes for garlic mashed potatoes and shoulder of mutton with garlic in her *Booke of Cookery,* a collection of family recipes, but the apogee of upper-class colonial cooking was found in the travels and kitchens of Thomas Jefferson. Jefferson was, by all accounts, America's first foodie. He spent five years in France and so warmly embraced its culinary traditions that he set up his slave James Hemings with French cooking lessons. Hemings would prepare the lavish feasts that Jefferson served in Paris and was granted his freedom after he taught everything he'd learned in France to the cooks at Monticello. Jefferson's Federalist opponent Joseph Dennie disparaged the president, decrying, "His principles relish so strongly of Paris, and are seasoned with such a profusion of French garlic, that he offends the whole nation."

Although records of Jefferson's White House dinners are surprisingly scarce (he wrote everything else down), we know that garlic figured heavily in the venison served at the president's table. When he retired to Monticello, Jefferson preferred vegetables to the more traditional meat and light French wine to George Washington's beloved sticky-sweet Madeira. In his Monticello garden, Jefferson grew over 250 vegetables, many of which were imported, including *aglio di Toscana* (Tuscan garlic), prompting Peter J. Hatch, who restored the garden, to declare it "an Ellis Island" of immigrant plants.

Mary Randolph, a well-born woman and cousin of Jefferson's, was the author of *The Virginia House-Wife* (1824), one of the best-known cookbooks of the time. Randolph was regarded as the best cook in Virginia. She routinely used garlic and several other herbs in her cooking, which embraced not only Virginian specialties but English, French, and Spanish cooking along with both East and West Indian curries. The French influence of former White House chef Honoré Julien and maitre d' Etienne Lamaire are likely responsible for the staggering (at the time) two heads of garlic in her Beef à la Mode. Randolph gave a copy of her book to Jefferson, and both his daughter and granddaughters regularly used more than forty of the recipes including a garlicky Beef Bouilli; the beef stewed in water with garlic and other vegetables was one of Jefferson's favorites. This glimpse into both Jefferson's gardens and Randolph's cookbook suggests that Virginians enjoyed more robust flavors than their New England and mid-Atlantic counterparts, but it was not to last. Thanks to the benumbing influence of the Puritans who believed that garlic was fit only for the Papist French and Italians, garlic went underground in North America for the next two hundred years.

Almost a century after Amelia Simmons disparaged garlic, Thomas De Voe, a New York butcher, reiterated her sentiments in his book, *The Market Assistant*. After defining garlic as "a species of the onion, with an acrimonious taste, and a most disagreeable smell," he also acknowledged the French connection, explaining, "It is much used by the French in a great many dishes for seasoning, soups, stews, and other dishes, and has also many medicinal qualities."

Despite its medical prowess, garlic's taste wasn't faring any better across the pond than it was on this side. Writing in her influential 1861 *Book of Household Management,* a guide to running a proper Victorian home, Isabella Beeton declared that "the smell of this plant is generally considered offensive." And one of my favorite recipes of all time is Mrs. W. G. Waters's Recipe No. 73 for Stufato alla Florentina (Stewed Beef), which was included in *The Cook's Decameron: A Study in Taste, Containing over Two Hundred Recipes for Italian Dishes* published in London in 1901. The recipe calls for a single clove of garlic with one cut that can be added for five minutes and then removed. It reminds me of the story of a famous chef who was said to chew a clove of garlic and then breathe on the food to impart its delicate flavor. In his essay *The English People,* George Orwell summed his people thus: "As a rule they will refuse even to sample a foreign dish, they regard such things as garlic and olive oil with disgust, life is unlivable to them unless they have tea and puddings."

COMING TO AMERICA: THE GARLIC IMMIGRATION

Garlic did start rumbling a bit in the American kitchens of the 1920s when salads became popular. The tremors started off gently; several recipes for salads published in *Good Housekeeping* during this time offered the following admonition to the cook: "Don't forget to rub the inside of the bowl with a clove of garlic (held on the tines of a fork) for delicious added flavor!" This advice was also popular across the pond and gave British food writer Elizabeth David the opportunity for a brilliant riposte: "The grotesque prudishness and archness with which garlic is treated in this country has led to the superstition that rubbing the bowl with it before putting the salad in gives sufficient flavor. It rather depends whether you're going to eat the bowl or the salad."

Plucked from the chorus, garlic played a starring role in the Caesar salad, perhaps the most famous salad in the world. Most historians agree that the Caesar salad was invented in Tijuana, Mexico, in 1924 by Caesar Cardini, an Italian immigrant. It was the Fourth of July weekend and Cardini's restaurant was low on food and expecting a rash of Yanks from over the border eager to celebrate the holiday without the inconvenience of Prohibition.

Cardini put together a salad from whatever he had in his kitchen and, to lessen the workload on his kitchen staff, created a dish that could be prepared tableside by waiters. The salad of Romaine lettuce topped with a dressing of crushed garlic, coddled eggs, olive oil, and Worcestershire sauce, sprinkled with Parmesan cheese and garlic-flavored croutons, was a smashing success (especially with Hollywood stars like Clark Gable and W. C. Fields who would flock to Tijuana to both elude Prohibition and enjoy the salad). Even Julia Child who, in one of her earliest remembrances, recalls driving from San Diego to Tijuana with her parents to partake of the salad, writes, "Two eggs in a salad? Two one-minute coddled eggs? And garlic-flavored croutons, and grated Parmesan cheese? It was a sensation of a salad from coast to coast, and there were even rumblings of its success in Europe." In the 1930s, the Caesar salad was voted by the master chefs of the International Society of Epicures in Paris as the "greatest recipe to originate from the Americas in fifty years."

Despite its breakout performance, garlic still had a ways to go to gain respectability. In *The Questing Cook,* published in 1927, Ruth A. Jeremiah Gottfried, opened her book by lamenting, "In America, the name of garlic is in bad odor. This conception is a libel upon garlic and upon the land of garlic eaters." The controversial author was, alas, ahead of her time.

Frank Capra's holiday classic *It's a Wonderful Life* illustrates the prejudicial attitudes that pertained to garlic eaters in mid-twentieth-century America. In the film, the town's most powerful banker, Mr. Potter, played by Lionel Barrymore, distrusts ethnic minorities and refers to the Italian community as "George Bailey's garlic eaters" after Jimmy Stewart's character gives loans to the town's immigrants. Even the Yankee Clipper, baseball great Joe DiMaggio (né Giuseppe Paolo DiMaggio, son of Sicilian immigrants), was not immune from the stereotype. A 1939 profile in *LIFE* magazine declared that the California-born slugger was "well-adapted to most US mores" and "used water instead of olive oil to slick his hair and never reeks of garlic."

Waverley Root, an American Paris-based news correspondent who became a noted food writer, chronicled garlic's gradual acceptance in the United States. In his essay collection, *Food,* Root wrote, "Before I left America for France in 1927, you were looked down upon if you ate garlic, and when I returned in 1940, you were looked down upon if you didn't." While garlic was gradually accepted in sophisticated kitchens in the 1940s where the cuisine of Provence had become fashionable, it wasn't really until the 1950s and 1960s that garlic arrived.

"In the beginning, there was Beard," Julia Child famously intoned. James Beard moved from Portland, Oregon, to New York in 1937 and after conceding that he would never be a great actor, opened a catering business, and started writing cookbooks. His casual, cheerful writing style veered from the workmanlike, home economics–tone of his predecessors. Beard loved food, wine, and entertaining, as evidenced by his 300-pound frame that Craig Claiborne described as "a giant panda, Santa Claus, and the Jolly Green Giant rolled into one."

During WWII, Beard was sent to Puerto Rico, Rio de Janeiro, Panama, and Marseilles as a member of the United Seamen's Service (USS), an organization set up to provide a "home away from home" for American sailors on shore leave. It was the perfect fit. In each city, Beard would hire local chefs and supervise the kitchen. His USS service introduced him to new cuisines, ingredients, and cooking methods, his time in Marseilles most especially. As his biographer Evan Jones writes, "It was the reality of Provence, with garlic as its essence, that lured him as nothing else every would." Beard was mesmerized by bouillabaisse, *brandade de morue* (salt cod and potatoes pureed with heavy cream and garlic), and *poulet aux senteurs de Provence* (chicken with lemon, basil, and garlic). Garlic was known as the truffle of Provence, and Beard returned from Marseilles with two garlicky recipes that would become his signatures. The first was his legendary Chicken with Forty Cloves of Garlic, a Provençal dish that Beard taught for years in his classes because "it never failed to astonish the students because the garlic becomes so mild and buttery when it's cooked through." (In *Masters of American Cookery,* Betty Fussell writes, "In the 1950s, calling for forty cloves of garlic in a single recipe was tantamount to joining the Communist Party.") Today, the recipe is a popular Passover dish with Jewish cooks who say that the forty cloves represent the Israelites' forty years of wandering.

The second recipe was Marseilles Garlic Soup made with thirty cloves of garlic and (in a perfect world) fat from chicken, goose, and pork. Fearing that his readers might replace fresh garlic with the more readily available garlic powder, he cautioned, "The robust and beautiful flavor of this soup is something that could never, ever be achieved with garlic powder. So leave those substitutes on the shelf, look at them once with distaste—and then forget about them." Thank you, James Beard.

In *Mastering the Art of French Cooking,* published in 1961, Julia Child and her co-authors, Simone Beck and Louisette Bertholle, introduced their readers to a bounty of pungent, garlicky fare unlikely to have graced America's suburban tables before. Suddenly, Westchester wives were whipping up Purée de Pommes de Terre à l'Ail (garlic mashed potatoes with thirty cloves of garlic) and Provençal classics like Poulet Sauté aux Herbes de Provence (chicken with herbs and garlic, egg yolk and butter sauce), Aioli (garlic mayonnaise), Aigo Bouido (garlic soup), and Bouillabaisse with Rouille (fish stew with a sauce of garlic, pimiento, and chili pepper). And Americans, who'd been serving roast leg of lamb with mint sauce since colonial times, were suddenly topping their lamb with Child's creamy garlic sauce made with a whole head of garlic.

While Child and Beard were revolutionizing home cooking in the United States, Elizabeth David was rousing the taste buds of war-weary palates in England. In 1950, she established garlic's foothold in England by publishing *A Book of Mediterranean Food,* which was hailed widely as "a garlic manifesto." In the book's introduction, David quotes French-born, London-based gastronome and cookbook author Marcel Boulestin: "It is not really an exaggeration to say that peace and happiness begin geographically, where garlic is used in cooking." So true.

Boulestin himself had written several cookbooks before David, in which he attempted to introduce the English to simple French cooking. They were very popular, but he treated his readers with kid gloves with recipes calling for "a tiny piece of garlic" or "a little [very little] chopped garlic." In one recipe, Boulestin even instructs his readers to "add parsley and garlic, omitting the garlic if you do not like the flavor."

When David's book first came out, the British still considered foreign cuisine "filthy," and the only place they could buy olive oil was in pharmacies, where it was marked "For External Use Only." Coming at the end of war-time rationing and just as exotic, Mediterranean ingredients like olive oil, saffron, basil, and yes, garlic were appearing on British shelves. The timing of *A Book of Mediterranean Food* was ideal.

David taught the British about such sun-kissed, garlicky delights as hummus, gazpacho, and ratatouille, and in so doing, she inspired British cooks Rose Gray and Ruth Rogers of London's iconic River Cafe and celebrity chefs Nigella Lawson and Jamie Oliver. David also made an indelible impression on Alice Waters who created Berkeley's legendary Chez Panisse. Waters was, and is, one of the country's fiercest champions of eating local, organic, and seasonal—and she was also one of the first restaurateurs to serve whole roasted heads of garlic.

The seeds of Chez Panisse were sown when Waters, a student at Berkeley, went to study abroad at the Sorbonne in Paris. There, she became obsessed with French food and first nursed the idea of opening a cafe. When Waters returned home, she decided to cook her way through David's *French Provincial Cooking* much the way the blogger Julie Powell later cooked her way through Julia Child's *Mastering the Art of French Cooking*. So there was "Alice and Elizabeth" long before blogging existed and "Julie and Julia" became a best-selling book and a Hollywood movie. Waters met her future mentor through their mutual friend, Richard Olney, the brilliant Iowa-born Francophile and author whose first cookbook, *The French Menu Cookbook*, was declared the best cookbook of all time by a panel of British chefs and food writers. (David's *French Provincial Cooking* was number two.) Without David and Olney, Waters would be the first to admit, there would be no Chez Panisse.

It's not surprising given her choice of mentors that Waters considers garlic "the spice of life" and would like her last meal to be garlic soup with family and friends. (Olney's recipe for rich garlic soup thickened with eggs and Parmesan cheese is one of the best ever put to paper and would make for an alliaceous send-off worthy of an Egyptian pharaoh.)

It's also not surprising that Waters and her comrades at Chez Panisse held the country's first garlic festival in 1975 while the rest of the country was embracing such culinary innovations as French's Onion Bits, Stove Top Stuffing, and Pop Rocks. The first festival was a weeklong affair that featured garlic in every savory dish. For her first outing, Waters didn't include garlic in dessert—serving only garlic-*shaped* meringues—but later garlic festival desserts included Orange Compote with Candied Lemon Rind and Garlic and garlic-infused wine fruit sorbets. The Chez Panisse garlic dinner has become a tradition and has been held annually on Bastille Day (July 14). Not coincidentally, the festival falls right in the middle of California's garlic harvest.

THE GREAT GARLIC PRESS CONTROVERSY

The debate over whether or not to use a garlic press is the culinary equivalent of the evolution debate. Tempers flare and opinions fly like edicts from warring gods. Advocates argue that a garlic press breaks more of the clove's cell walls, giving the garlic a lighter, more delicate flavor. The editors at *Cook's Illustrated* believe that "a good garlic press can break down cloves more finely and evenly than an average cook using a knife, which means better distribution of garlic flavor throughout any given dish." In *Mastering the Art of French Cooking*, Julia Child declared the garlic press a "wonderful invention." Discussing how to make garlic puree in *In Julia's Kitchen with Master Chefs,* she writes, "The garlic press will do the job, but a garlic press, at least among certain of the food cognoscenti, is absolutely a no-no-non-object used only by non-people and non-cooks. Thus it behooves us all to know of and to be able to execute this perfect hand technique, which actually is fast and easy when you have several cloves of garlic that need the treatment."

The opponents of the garlic press are a more vociferous bunch. Not surprisingly, Anthony Bourdain has strong feelings about the press as well as the criminal misuse of garlic. He called garlic presses "disgusting abominations" and said "I don't know what that junk is that squeezes out of the end of those things, but it ain't garlic." Iron Chef Michael Symon admits he wants to "kill the guy who invented the garlic press," and Alice Waters sees no reason to waste money on a garlic press or any other fancy gadgets. She recommends using a mortar and pestle to make a garlic puree and offers "The French Grandmother's Fork Method": Press the tines of a fork against a cutting board—then, rub a garlic clove back and forth over the tines to make a quick garlic paste. When I was growing up, my mother told me that *New York Times* food critic and cookbook author Craig Claiborne was anti–garlic press, claiming it produced a bitter garlic. Writing in a 1986 issue of *Tatler* magazine, Elizabeth David devoted an entire essay to the press called "Garlic Presses Are Utterly Useless." Food Network star and culinary geek Alton Brown echoes David, declaring them "utterly, completely, magnificently useless." He goes on, "I'd go further than that. I regard garlic presses as both ridiculous and pathetic, their effect being precisely the reverse of what people who buy them believe will be the case. Squeezing the juice out of garlic doesn't reduce its potency; it concentrates it and intensifies the smell."

~ Garlic of a Different Stripe

Garlic turns green or blue when the sulfur compounds that give garlic its pungent flavor react with each other and natural amino acids to produce harmless green- or blue-tinted pigments. Green-colored garlic is stronger than white garlic because it contains more of the aromatic sulfuric compounds. These pigments are chemically related to chlorophyll, the molecules that give leaves their green color. Garlic can also form its own chlorophyll if it's stored in light. Chlorophyll is harmless, but it will make garlic bitter, so it's best to store garlic in a dark, aerated place.

Aged garlic is more likely to change color than fresh garlic. Onions have some of the same compounds as garlic—and when onions and garlic are cooked together, they frequently turn a turquoise-blue color. (This is one of the reasons that Indian cooks

continued

don't grind garlic and onions together and that they cook onions first, and then add garlic.) Another way to keep garlic from turning a color is to avoid adding an acid like vinegar at the beginning of cooking as it may activate the chemical reaction.

While most people want to avoid colored garlic, people in northern China make a special green-tinted garlic called Laba Garlic, which is believed to be auspicious and is served during New Year's celebrations. To make your own Laba Garlic, age three heads of garlic for several months. Peel the garlic and place the cloves in a jar with a lid. Add one tablespoon of sugar and one cup of rice vinegar. Seal the jar and place it in a cold dark place for two weeks, after which the garlic will have turned green. Laba Garlic is served with Chinese dumplings.

The garlic-loving Koreans developed black garlic, a genetically unique six-clove garlic that mystics claimed would give women supernatural powers and immortality. Today, although the immortality claim is suspect, black garlic is still cultivated using an ancient botanical process. To make it, garlic is placed in earthenware jugs in a cool environment where it is left to age for several months. The blackened cloves have a unique sweet flavor like roasted garlic marinated in balsamic vinegar. Black garlic is prized for its complex, subtle umami taste, the fifth taste (alongside sweet, sour, bitter, and salty). *Umami* translates as "savory deliciousness" and is known for its ability to expand and complement the flavor of other ingredients.

Black garlic is also popular in Japan where it's fermented in the northern prefecture of Aomori. Ferran Adrià discovered black garlic while traveling in Japan and became one of its earliest proponents at his culinary shrine El Bulli. A black olive turned out to be an illusion crafted of pure black garlic, and a black-colored tomato was covered with a coating made of black garlic pureed in thick oil. Recently in Barcelona, Adrià's brother opened a Peruvian-Japanese fusion restaurant called Pakta where one of the signature dishes is Nobu-Style Grilled Black Cod in a Black Garlic–Miso Marinade.

Black garlic became an American foodie favorite in 2009 and it continues to attract the attention of innovative American chefs. While the ancient manufacturing process is a closely guarded secret, manufacturers and chefs are cooking up their own secret recipes. Chef Evan Hanczor of Brooklyn's Parish Hall makes his own black garlic and explains its unique appeal. "It's deep. The flavors are so layered, and they linger. It has notes of dark caramel, chocolate, a little bitterness, a little sweetness, and umami, plus that *je ne sais quoi.*" Hanczor serves Celery Root Baked in a Salt Crust with Black Garlic Sauce, Almond, Cocoa Nib, and Rosemary. At Blanca, also in Brooklyn, Pastry Chef Katy Peetz serves a gremolata-inspired Parsley Cake, Fennel–Black Garlic Gelato, Meyer Lemon Granita, and Parsley–Olive Oil Crumble. According to Peetz, "[Black garlic] brings an almost disturbing but lovely characteristic to the dish that people don't usually associate with dessert."* Chef Eric Ripert of Le Bernardin was an early fan and continues to use black garlic in his delicate, delicious seafood preparations. Flash Marinated Hamachi is served over a Black Garlic–Ponzu Sauce, and Charred Octopus comes with an umami-intensive Green Olive and Black Garlic Emulsion.

* Caroline Hatchett, "The Dirty Secrets and Deep Flavor of Black Garlic," StarChefs.com online magazine (March 2013): www.starchefs.com/cook/savory/product/black-garlic.

When Chris Cosentino of San Francisco's Incanto competed against Mario Batali on *Iron Chef*'s "Battle Garlic," he cooked up a pork belly braised with eighty cloves of garlic that was served with duck fat–fried tripe atop creamy polenta. Some people think Americans have gone too far in jumping on the garlic bandwagon, and that includes the late, great Marcella Hazan. Hazan has been widely regarded as the Julia Child of Italian cooking since the 1973 publication of her legendary first book, *The Classic Italian Cookbook*. When asked what's wrong with Italian cooking in America today, Hazan declared, "Too much garlic, too little salt, and much of what's on the menu at Olive Garden."

Actually, the folks at the Olive Garden, who start every meal with garlic-butter breadsticks, might be on to more than Hazan realized. In a 2000 study titled "Effects of Garlic Bread on Family Interactions," Dr. Alan Hirsch, neurological director of the Smell and Taste Treatment and Research Foundation, reported that the smell of garlic bread enhanced positive family interactions by 25 percent and decreased negative interactions by 23 percent.

NEVER IN BAD TASTE: COPING WITH GARLIC BREATH

What book on garlic would neglect to address the most common "affliction" of garlic lovers, garlic breath? While some garlic lovers consider garlic breath a badge of honor, this section is for those who don't. Here are some of the most common ways to eliminate garlic breath.

Chewing gum stimulates saliva in the mouth, reducing bad breath; the extra saliva rinses away bacteria and volatile sulfur compounds. Essential oils may also kill germs that can cause bad breath, so look out for chewing gums and mouthwashes that contain cinnamon, peppermint, and spearmint oils, which are especially effective (and taste good too). Thanks to their citric acid, slices of apple, orange, lemon, or melon eaten after a garlicky dinner will also keep the mouth moist with saliva.

Green and black teas have powerful antioxidants called polyphenols that inhibit the growth of bacteria and may suppress the sulfuric compounds that garlic produces. Other plant chemicals like chlorophyll bind to the sulfuric compounds in garlic and help neutralize odor. Basil, thyme, cilantro, mint, dill, and parsley have similar effects.

Sheryl Barringer and Areerat Hansanugrum, researchers in the Department of Food Science and Technology at Ohio State University, found that a mixture of fat and water is the best way to deodorize garlic's volatile compounds, making milk a potent weapon against garlic breath. Thanks to its fat content, drinking whole milk is better than drinking skim milk or water alone. The researchers point out that adding milk to garlic before eating it is better at deodorizing the volatile compounds than drinking milk after eating garlic. Six ounces of yogurt have also been found to combat garlic breath by reducing hydrogen sulfide. Barringer also says that apples, basil, spinach, and parsley will reduce garlic breath—but only, she advises, "when they're mixed with garlic."

Mustard that contains the spice turmeric can help eliminate garlic breath because turmeric contains the antioxidant chemical curcumin. (Warning: This works, but it's a bit of a rough ride even if, like me, you love mustard.) Swirl a teaspoon of mustard around your mouth for a minute, then spit it out. After that, swallow half a teaspoon of mustard to kill the bacteria in your stomach. As an added bonus, curcumin is anti-inflammatory and believed to have cancer-preventing and memory-boosting properties. Curcumin is popular in Indian food, and some scientists think it might help to explain the low incidence of dementia in India.

Swishing instant coffee around your mouth and spitting it out also works, and since roasted coffee beans have antibacterial properties, chewing on them eliminates bad breath. Drinking strong coffee reduces garlic breath, but only if you leave out the cream and sugar which can increase odor from bacteria.

Nibbling on whole allspice, cloves, cinnamon sticks, cardamom pods, and fennel seeds reduces bad breath because they contain the compound eugenol, the active ingredient in clove oil. (Garlic-hating Puritans used to chew fennel seeds, which they called "meeting seeds." It was said that they used them as an appetite suppressant, but they may also have used them to cover up the smell of the forbidden nips of whiskey they drank before their lengthy church services.) A slice of bread can also reduce garlic breath because, as any Atkins dieter knows, a lack of carbs contributes to bad breath.

Water mixed with half a teaspoon of vinegar or baking soda also does the trick, but leaving the best for last: alcohol kills bacteria and combats garlic breath. Vodka is the most popular choice as it doesn't have a lingering aftertaste. Otherwise, you risk replacing garlic breath with alcohol breath. You can either down a shot or enjoy a vodka cocktail (but avoid sugary cocktails as the sugar aggravates halitosis). You can also make your own mouthwash from one cup of vodka and nine tablespoons of ground cinnamon. The mixture should be allowed to sit for two weeks so the cinnamon can thoroughly infuse the vodka. (This also makes a lovely nightcap.)

three

HIGH STAKES AND LOVE CHARMS:
GARLIC IN LEGEND AND LORE

*Following the Rumanian tradition, garlic is used in excess to
keep vampires away; following the Jewish tradition, a dispenser
of schmaltz (liquid chicken fat) is kept on the table to give the
vampires heartburn if they get through the garlic defense.*

—Calvin Trillin, *Alice, Let's Eat*

Garlic has been credited with powers of both good and evil throughout history. It's been associated with the devil and used by witches to
cast evil spells. On the flip side, it's been a source of luck and protected
both people and animals from demons, witches, the evil eye, the plague,
vampires, and the occasional troll. Garlic bulbs have been used in bridal
bouquets and love potions as well as to send unrequited lovers packing.

THE DEVIL AND MORAL CORRUPTION

Mohammed equated garlic with Satan when he described the feet
of the devil as he was cast out of the Garden of Eden. The prophet
claimed that garlic sprang up from where Satan placed his left foot and
onion sprouted from where he placed his right one. While Mohammed

appreciated the medicinal effects of garlic, he did not want its odor permeating mosques and issued four *hadith* (sayings) to that effect. In the Islamic faith, garlic is considered a *khabith* (that which is impure, base, and wicked). The prophet declared, "He who has eaten [raw] onion or garlic or leek should not approach our mosque, because the angels are also offended by the strong smells that offend the children of Adam." If garlic has been boiled to such an extent that the odor vanishes, its use is permitted. And should the Messenger of Allah happen to find a man with such offensive odor in the mosque, he would order him to be taken out of the mosque and sent to Al-Baqi—the cemetery! Today, Mohammed would have to send entire countries to the cemetery as the smell of garlic wafts out of the thousands of falafel and hummus stands that dot the street corners of the Middle East.

The idea that bad smells are associated with moral corruption and good smells with moral rectitude appears frequently throughout history. The devil has been known for his sulfurous aroma since, as it's written in the Book of Revelation, he was cast into a lake of fire and brimstone for all eternity. Brimstone is the ancient name for sulfur and sulfuric compounds, which are, of course, also responsible for garlic's odor. The devil was an amorphous concept until 447 C.E. when the Council of Toledo led by Pope Leo I was the first to describe his physical manifestation: a large, black, horned apparition with cloven hoofs, an immense phallus, and a sulfurous stench.

While sweet smells were considered conducive to healthy living and safe food preparation, bad smells indicated the presence of disease, decay, decadence, and death. Puritan minister Thomas Manton spoke of those who "have no affection to spiritual and heavenly things; like the rebellious Israelites, who more desired the onions and garlic of Egypt than the milk and honey of the promised land." The medieval concept of the *foetor Judaicus* (Jewish stink) linked the sulfurous devil to the base, garlic-smelling Jews and differentiated them from the pure, sweet-smelling (and baptized) Christians. During this period, the German cities of Speyer, Worms, and Mainz were the most important communities of Jewish education in the Holy Roman Empire. The three cities were known collectively as Shum (Hebrew for garlic), which was formed from the first letters of the Hebrew town names. Thirteenth-century Austrian poet Seifried Helbling claimed that "there was never a state so large that a mere thirty Jews would not saturate it with stench and unbelief." Some believed that converting to Christianity and being baptized could purify Jews and vanquish their "inherent bad smell."*

⌁Garlic and Anti-Semitism

As the menace of anti-Semitism in Germany and beyond grew throughout the nineteenth and early twentieth centuries, the Nazis called on science to explain "the smell of the Jew." "The Racial Biology of the Jews" was published during the Third Reich, in 1938, by Baron Otmar von Verschuer, MD, former head of the Kaiser Wilhelm Institute. In the periodical *Forschungen fur Judenfrage* ("Research on the Jewish Problem"), Verschuer wrote of the scent of garlic emitted by the Jews through the apocrine glands which "are supposed to be present to a greater extent among the colored races and the Jews, especially of the female sex." The garlic plant was so indelibly associated with Jews that the Nazis issued buttons with pictures of garlic bulbs so wearers could broadcast their ardent anti-Semitism. According to historian Mark Graubard, "The mere mention of garlic by a Nazi orator caused the crowd to howl with fury and hatred."

The consumption of garlic was even used by Sephardic Jews (from Andalusia) to disparage the Ashkenazi Jews of northern Europe. Maimonides, a rabbi who lived until 1204 and is widely considered the greatest medieval Jewish philosopher, wrote in a letter to his son,

---

* See, for example, Rabbi Israel Levi's article "Le Juif de la légende" in *Revue des Études Juives*, 1890.

"Guard your soul by not looking into books composed by Ashkenazi rabbis, who believe in God only when they eat beef seasoned with vinegar and garlic. They believe that the vapors of vinegar and garlic will ascend to their nostrils and thus make them understand that God is near them. . . . You, my son, should stay only in the pleasant company of our Sephardi brothers . . . because only they have brains and are clever." Maimonides adopted nine out of ten of the prophet Ezra's ordinances; not surprisingly, he left out the one that encouraged eating garlic on the sabbath.

Garlic's link with the underworld and moral depravity can be found in other religious traditions throughout the world. Priests in ancient Greece would not permit anyone who had eaten garlic to enter the Temple of Cybele (a fertility goddess). Garlic was considered the sacred plant of the dark goddess Hecate and was part of ritual known as "Hecate's supper." Three-headed statues of Hecate were placed at crossroads where people could leave offerings of garlic to seek her protection in their travels, as well as to distract any demons that might be following them. The offering was to be made in the middle of the night, on the eve of the full moon. One was to place the garlic at a pile of stones, leave the site quickly, and not look back. (As Hecate was usually accompanied by red-eyed hell hounds and an entourage of dead people, this was probably for the best.)

SLAYER OF MONSTERS

While garlic's strong sulfurous smell links it to the devil, its smell is also one of several reasons garlic is considered apotropaic, meaning it has the power to ward off evil spirits. In ancient Sanskrit texts, garlic was referred to as a "slayer of monsters" as it has long been protecting people from witchcraft, demons, and evil spirits. In ancient Egypt, garlic's curative powers were widely valued, and from there, its reputation spread throughout Europe and beyond, and it became renowned for its ability to protect people from supernatural forces as well. Since it wasn't yet clear why garlic worked, its powers were attributed to magic. In ancient Greece, upper-class citizens considered garlic's taste vulgar, but it was esteemed for its powers of protection against witches, sorcerers, and savage bulls. Expectant parents would hang garlic in delivery rooms and on their newborn's crib to protect the child from witches. In Homer's *Odyssey*, garlic protects Odysseus from the sorceress Circe, who turns his non-garlic-eating companions into pigs, while in the *Argonautica*, Medea smothers her beloved Jason and his weapons with garlic to protect him from her father's fire-breathing bulls.

During medieval times, illness was often considered a manifestation of evil, and since herbal remedies were linked to good spirits, they were seen as a potent weapon against the forces of darkness. Garlic's purifying properties were also attributed to its strong odor, and it was believed that garlic could drive out the body's evil humors, which were thought to cause illness.

Henry IV of France was baptized with garlic to protect him from disease, as well as from evil spirits, precipitating a lifelong love affair with garlic. The king, nicknamed Le Roi d'Ail, supposedly ate so many cloves every day that he exuded garlic from every pore and one of his contemporaries claimed that his breath could "fell an ox at twenty paces." Given his amorous proclivities with both wives and mistresses, one can only hope that the ladies of the court appreciated garlic's alleged aphrodisiacal properties more than they deprecated its smell.

In ancient times, Koreans ate pickled garlic before passing through the mountains to keep tigers away as they believed that tigers hated the smell, and Africans used garlic to repel crocodiles. (I've found no evidence that garlic repels either tigers or crocodiles and have no inclination to test this hypothesis.) German miners took garlic down the mineshaft to protect themselves from evil spirits, and Spanish bullfighters carried cloves of garlic into the ring for protection against agitated bulls.

The ancient belief that garlic fumes could destroy a compass's magnetism led sailors to believe that garlic protected them from shipwrecks and persisted until the early seventeenth century. While he'd heard reports of British helmsmen being flogged for eating garlic, scholar Giambattista della Porta asked mariners if it was true that they were forbidden to eat onions and garlic. They told him that not only was that an old wives' tale, but that men of the sea would sooner lose their lives than abstain from eating onions and garlic.

Warding Off the Evil Eye

Throughout the world, garlic is believed to ward off the evil eye, a malevolent look from someone who is jealous, envious, or covetous that's said to bring on illness or bad luck. It's widely believed that beautiful children attract the evil eye, so throughout the Mediterranean—where the belief in the evil eye is especially strong—mothers carry garlic in their pockets or handbags to protect their children. If the child of a Sephardic Jew is complimented, her mother would say, "Let it go to the garlic." There's even a Turkish saying, "Garlic and cloves! Keep the Evil Eye away! The sooner the better!" which I'm assuming sounds better in Turkish.

Attracting Luck

Garlic continues to be used in the present day to bring good luck and better fortune. European runners believe that rubbing garlic on their bodies before a race keeps competitors from catching up. In Hungary, jockeys rub their horses with garlic, believing that the smell repels the other horses so the jockey and his garlic-scented steed might sail across the finish line. And cab drivers in Belize place cloves of garlic on their dashboard to attract both good luck and money. Dreaming that there's garlic in the house is supposedly lucky, while to dream about eating garlic suggests that you are giving your luck away. Some believe that if a young woman dreams of eating garlic, she is looking to marry for security rather than for love. And to dream that you are walking through a garlic patch suggests that you will rise from poverty to prosperity. (Note to self: Dream about walking through a garlic patch.)

Expressing Love

The earliest bridal bouquets and wreaths included garlic bulbs to ward off ever-present evil spirits. The first use of wedding flowers was in ancient Greece, where brides wore a crown of flowers, herbs, and garlic bulbs. In ancient Rome, both the bride and groom wore garlands of strong-smelling flowers, garlic, and herbs around their necks to symbolize long life and fertility, and during medieval times when plagues ravaged Europe, brides would clutch bouquets of garlic and herbs over their mouths and noses to keep disease away. Today, it's traditional for a Palestinian bridegroom to wear a clove of garlic in his buttonhole to be assured of a successful wedding night, and Swedish bridegrooms sew a clove of garlic and a sprig of rosemary in their clothes to avert the evil eye.

In the repressive Victorian era, men and women sent flowers to each other to communicate their private feelings. Garlic must have confused people, as it signified everything from courage, strength, and protection to "What I feel for you is utmost indifference," "I can't stand you," and "I think you're evil." A garlic-rose perfume sold at the Gilroy Garlic Festival was promoted with the following tagline: "He may forget your name, but he'll know you've been there."

There's a gypsy love spell that calls for a lovesick person to plant garlic in a red clay pot while repeating the name of the person they desire. Every day at sunrise and sunset, the person should water the plant and recite the following incantation: "As this root grows, let the heart of (insert name here) turn unto me." A variation of this spell calls for the spell caster to include a drop of his or her own blood.

If the spell works but you get tired of your conquest, you can use this method to get rid of a former flame: Stick two crossed pins in a garlic bulb and place it at a crossroads. Lure the unrequited lover to the spot, and when he or she crosses it, they will lose interest. If you want to take things a little further and bring evil upon someone, a witch doctor can prepare a formula using a photograph of the person, hair from a black cat, sand from the cemetery, and garlic. Bury the concoction in a place your intended victim frequently walks and the evil spell will take hold.

WARDING OFF VAMPIRES AND OTHER EVILS

Garlic has been used to repel and destroy vampiric demons throughout the world for over two thousand years. There are two kinds of vampires: bloodsucking vampires and psychic vampires who suck out their victim's life force. Best known are the bloodsuckers who hail from Central and Eastern Europe. Their place in folklore was probably spread by the bands of gypsies who traveled throughout the region in the early eighteenth century. Outbreaks of vampire hysteria in Europe frequently coincided with outbreaks of the plague. Since people had no explanation for why friends and family were dropping dead around them, they ascribed the plague to superstitious agents like witches, werewolves, vampires, and other supernatural demons. Garlic's healthy, curative properties must have seemed anathema to undead vampires. Garlic was also used to repel bloodsucking mosquitoes, and as diseases caused by mosquito bites were considered "the touch of the vampire," garlic could logically be assumed to repel bloodsucking vampires as well. Some have also equated vampirism with rabies. People with rabies have a heightened sense of smell that would have been offended by the strong aroma of garlic.

As Mark Jenkins discussed in *Vampire Forensics,* there was also little understanding of what happened to the human body after death. The dead were buried in mass graves, which frequently had to be reopened to bury more victims. Corpses weren't yet embalmed, so when the graves were reopened, people saw bodies that were decomposing, grossly deformed, and dripping with blood. In their horror, they feared the dead had become vampires. If a dead person was thought to be in danger of becoming a vampire, their mouth was stuffed with garlic to prevent evil spirits from entering the dead body.

In Romania, the legendary home of Dracula, garlic is eaten frequently and used in several vampire-repelling rituals. People smear garlic on the windows and doors of their houses, on the gates of their farmyards, and even on the horns of their animals. Garlic is especially important on those days when vampire activity is believed to be greatest: St. Andrew's Eve, St. George's Eve, New Year's Eve, and Pentecost.

St. Andrew is the patron saint of wolves, Romania, and Scotland, as well as the protector against wolf attacks and the purported donor of garlic to humanity. St. Andrew's Eve (November 29), the most significant folkloric holiday of the year in Romania, is known as the Night of the Vampires, as it's believed that the barrier between the visible and the invisible world disappears, allowing ghosts and spirits to pass through. To protect themselves, people eat a lot of garlic and spread garlic paste in the shape of a crucifix on the front door. At night, there's a big party known as the Guarding the Garlic Party. The house selected to host the party is prepared in advance by smearing garlic around all the doors and windows. Every young woman brings three garlic bulbs to the party. The bulbs are collected and placed in a pot that's guarded by candlelight by (for some reason) the oldest woman in the house. The young people dance until dawn, when the pot is taken outside and the young men and women resume dancing around it. When they finish, the garlic is given out and taken home where it becomes a "sacred symbol" that protects the inhabitants against illness or evil spells. A young woman who wishes to attract suitors on this night is advised to wear a garlic belt around her waist.

On St. Andrew's Day, children in Transylvanian villages are told by their mothers to eat garlic in the morning and recite the following: "Garlic is shaped in the form of a cross; I have a cross on my forehead." This incantation is meant to ward off evil charms and spells that have been directed at the child. Young women gather in the house of one of the girls. Each of them bakes a knot-shaped bread, known as Andrew's Bread. When the bread has cooled down, each young woman places a garlic clove in the middle. If the garlic rises, it's a sign that she will soon be courted by a young man and will have luck in her marriage.

St. George is the patron saint of England, farmers, cows, and incongruously, syphilis. He's also known for his fight with the dragon which is widely interpreted as a battle with the devil. On St. George's Eve (April

22), evil spirits run wild and it's said that if the roaming ghosts are mildly malevolent, they steal fruit from the orchards and milk from the cows. If they are particularly mean, they steal people's minds. To keep evil spirits away, garlic is smeared on doors and windows; the garlic also keeps witches from sneaking through the cracks. Cows are also rubbed down with garlic and fed it in their food.

Continuing the theme, on New Year's Eve, Romanians burn bad-smelling objects and smear garlic on themselves, their family, their animals, and their doorsills to repel evil spirits. During Pentecost, garlic and wormwood are used to both prevent and treat illnesses caused by dangerous fairies who are said to be especially active during this time.

While the most commonly known way of becoming a vampire is to be bitten by another vampire, one can also become a vampire by dying an unnatural death (such as by suicide) or having an improper burial. During the Romanian Revolution of 1989, the corpse of Nicolae Ceausescu did not receive a proper burial, which made superstitious Romanians fear that he would become a vampire. To prevent this, revolutionary leader Gelu Voican carpeted the late dictator's apartment with braids of garlic.

⌒ Vampire Research

A group of Norwegian researchers wanted to test the hypothesis that garlic is an effective prophylactic against vampires. "Owing to the lack of vampires," they used leeches instead. The leeches preferred a hand covered with garlic to a clean hand, causing the doctors to recommend restrictions on the use of garlic in Norway. The same scientists later did a study entitled "Effect of Ale, Garlic, and Soured Cream on the Appetite of Leeches." In the nineteenth century, German doctors used all three of these to stimulate the appetite of leeches who weren't "cooperating" in bloodsucking. It turns out sour cream doesn't stimulate their appetite, ale makes them drunk, and garlic kills them.

Garlic has been used both to find vampires as well as to prevent vampires. A vampire in disguise could be spotted by not being willing to eat garlic. As recently as thirty years ago, a Romanian church distributed garlic during service, observing those who refused to eat it to see if the person was a vampire. (No one wrote about whether or not any vampires were discovered.)

A World of Vampires

While garlic-fearing vampires are especially prevalent in Romania, there are garlic-averse vampires throughout the world. International blood-suckers include the Asema, a vampire in Suriname folklore that walks around in human disguise during the day, but at night, it sheds its skin and turns into a large ball of blue light and sucks the blood of its victims. To protect themselves against the Asema, people eat garlic and bitter herbs that will taint their blood, making it unpalatable to the vampire.

The Philippine Aswang is a female vampire that also appears to be a normal human during the day, but at night, but she shape-shifts into an animal with a long, thin tongue. She inserts her tongue through cracks in the roof and sucks the blood of sleeping children. If an Aswang licks your shadow, you will die soon. To protect their children, Philippine parents rub garlic on their children's armpits.

Another female Philippine vampire, the Manananggal (one who severs), is an older, beautiful woman who severs her upper torso at night and flies with huge bat-like wings to prey on unsuspecting pregnant women, sucking out the hearts of fetuses or the blood of sleeping victims. She hates the smell of garlic, and one way to kill her is to pour garlic, salt, or ash on the severed bottom of the torso so she can't rejoin her upper part to it and dies at daybreak.

In Austria, Germany, and Bosnia-Herzegovina, one becomes a Blut-sauger (bloodsucker) by eating the flesh of any animal that was slaughtered by a wolf. To keep a Blutsauger from entering the house, one must daub all the doorways and windows with a paste made from mashed garlic and a distillate of hawthorn flowers. To kill a Blutsauger, people surround its coffin and dump baskets of garlic into it, which immobilizes the demon. Then, someone drives a stake of sharp hawthorn through the demon's stomach, pinning it to the coffin. After the Blutsauger is beheaded, its mouth is filled with more fresh garlic, its head is put in the coffin backward (facing hell), and the garlic-filled coffin is resealed and reburied.

The Portuguese Bruxa (Bruja in Mexico and other South American countries) is a female witch who worships Satan, feeds on the blood of children, and is said to be indestructible. A Bruxa doesn't like garlic, so parents sew garlic into their children's clothing to keep her from carrying them away.

The Dakhanavar is a vampire in Armenian folklore that protects the valley around Mount Ararat from intruders. Since the demon is said to stalk his prey, travelers carry cloves of garlic in their pockets and mashed garlic paste on their shoes. The Dakhanavar typically attacks his victims in their sleep and sucks the blood from their feet, so travelers who are camping outside roast entire garlic bulbs in the flames of their campfire. The combination of garlic and fire keeps the Dakhanavar away.

The Tlahuelpuchi (which means glowing haze or illuminated youth) is a shape-shifting vampire from the rural Mexican state of Tlaxcala that takes on a glowing aura when it's active. It is born with its affliction, which manifests itself during puberty, and is usually female. A Tlahuelpuchi must feed on human blood once a month or die. Their ideal victim is a child between three and six months old, but no younger. Garlic, onions, and metal repel the Tlahuelpuchi, but the only way to stop her is to kill her (which is accomplished most easily by denying her blood).

Energy Vampires

In contrast to bloodsucking vampires, psychic vampires feed off the life force of other human beings. In ancient Greece, Callicantzaros were humans born between Christmas and New Year's Day who become half-human, half-animal vampires after they die. Callicantzaros' are only active from Christmas to New Year's, when they destroy property and steal the souls of newborn children (to create more of themselves). Parents protected their infants by covering them with garlic sachets and burning a log that irritates the Callicantzaros, acute sense of smell. To prevent infants from turning into Callicantzaros, parents bound them in garlic tresses or singed their toenails (ouch).

Chiang-shih (Chinese vampires known as hopping corpses) are blind, reanimated corpses who kill living creatures to steal their energy (qi). They have trouble walking because of the pain and stiffness of being dead, so they hop. Since they're blind, you can evade them by holding your breath, as the only way they can detect their victims is from their breathing. People use garlic and salt to protect themselves from Chiang-shih.

In the Malay mythology of Southeast Asia, a Toyol is a small child spirit that a shaman creates from a dead human fetus using black magic. Toyols are usually used to steal things from other people. The nice thing about Toyols is that they're pretty stupid and you can distract them with braids of garlic, which the Toyol will start playing with until it forgets what it came to do.

Vampire Hunters

Vampire hunters and slayers specialize in tracking down and destroying vampires and other supernatural demons. Dhampirs are half-human, half-vampire creatures who have most of a vampire's powers but few of its weaknesses. They often reject their vampire blood and become very successful vampire hunters, but they share a regular vampire's fear of garlic. The Marvel Comics character Blade is a Dhampir who uses vampire mace, a serum made from garlic essence and silver nitrate, to repel vampires. Blade's mentor, Whistler, who made the serum, also injects it into Blade's colleague Dr. Karen Jenson just after she's bitten by a rogue vampire. Although she ultimately turns into a vampire herself, Karen nonetheless kills the evil vampire Mercury by spraying the serum into Mercury's mouth, causing her to explode.

The most famous (pre-Buffy) vampire hunter/slayer is Abraham

Van Helsing from Bram Stoker's novel *Dracula,* who is called on to save Lucy Westenra from the Transylvanian Count Dracula. The Dutch doctor orders garlic flowers sent from the Netherlands and fills her room with them. Van Helsing also drapes a wreath of garlic around Lucy's neck. Unfortunately, during the night, Lucy's mother removes all the "horrible, strong-smelling flowers," so Dracula returns to drain her blood. Lucy dies and shortly after her death, there are reports of a beautiful woman haunting young children. Van Helsing and Lucy's suitors track her down, stake her heart, behead her, and fill her mouth with garlic.

In the 1964 movie *The Last Man on Earth* (adapted from Richard Matheson's apocalyptic novel, *I Am Legend*), a solitary Vincent Price wakes up in the morning, gets dressed, has breakfast, opens his front door, and pulls a wreath of garlic and a broken mirror from his windows. "I'll need to replace these," he says in voice-over. When he walks out his front door, the lawn and driveway are strewn with corpses. A plague has turned all the humans on earth into vampires and Price is the last man standing. After picking up more garlic and a new mirror, he spends the day collecting corpses, driving stakes through their hearts, and throwing them into a burning pit on the edge of town. Just before nightfall, he drives back to his house, places the new garlic and mirror on the windows ("They are allergic to garlic and hate to look at their reflection," he explains), and settles down to dinner. Just another day as the last man on earth.

Stephen King also placed vampires in contemporary society in his second novel, *'Salem's Lot,* in which vampires take over a small town in Maine. King kept the traditional vampire repellents (garlic, crucifixes, holy water, roses). Increasingly, however, contemporary vampire-story authors are dismissive of the relationship between garlic and vampires. It appears in the first episode of the 1997–2003 television show, *Buffy the Vampire Slayer,* when we see Buffy's trunk of vampire repellents, which includes stakes, crosses, holy water, and garlic. In another episode, Buffy surrounds herself with garlic to protect herself from the vampire Spike. Spike and his rival for Buffy's affections, Angel, are both examples of Stregoni Benefici, good vampires who have repented, were brought back into the fold of the church by a priest, and now fight against evil vampires. (Stregoni Benefici are popular contemporary heroes probably because they're good "bad boys," as exemplified by Edward Cullen in the *Twilight* series.) In an episode that explores what Sunnydale would have been like if Buffy had never come to town and vampires were allowed to run rampant, the lockers of Sunnydale High are shown lined with braids of garlic.

Anne Rice, author of *The Vampire Chronicles,* decided that traditional vampire deterrents such as garlic, crosses, and wooden stakes wouldn't bother her characters. In an interview with *The Daily Beast,* Rice said, "I thought if they responded hysterically to garlic or crucifixes, that was not as interesting as their being nihilistic and atheistic, and not having a 'magical' response to something but having definite limitations and rules."

Stephenie Meyer, the writer of the *Twilight* series, also decided at the outset that her stories would have no fangs, no coffins, no stakes through the heart, and no garlic. In an interview, Meyer explained, "Almost all of the superstitions about vampire limitations are entirely

⌒ Vampire-Killing Kits

During the early nineteenth century, vampire-killing kits were all the rage. One such kit was a wooden box that came with a pistol, a silver bullet, a large bottle of holy water, small bottles of garlic juice (to coat the bullets), a special anti-vampire serum, sulfur powder, a crucifix, smelling salts to revive those who fainted during the vampire killing, and a copy of the 1819 book *History of Phantoms and Demons,* by Gabrielle de Paban. The label on the case said, "This box contains the items considered necessary for persons who travel into certain little known countries of Eastern Europe where the populace are plagued with a manifestation of evil known as vampires." The kit sold for $12,000 at Sotheby's on October 30, 2003.

false in my world. Vampires don't really have any limits, other than the self-imposed guideline to keep their existence a secret. No unconscious periods, no problem with sunlight, crosses, garlic, holy water, wooden stakes, etc. . . . These are all myths—deliberately placed in earlier centuries to mislead impressionable humans and make them feel safe."

four

GROWING YOUR OWN

There are five elements: earth, air, fire, water, and garlic.
Without garlic, I simply would not care to live.

—Louis Diat, chef de cuisine of the Ritz-Carlton Hotel
in New York for forty-one years

Garlic takes its name from the Anglo-Saxon words *gar* (spear) and *leac* (leak) because of its sharp, tapering leaves. After years of being considered a lily, garlic, was recently reclassified as a member of the amaryllis family.[*]

There are over 200 varieties of garlic, including the prized rose garlic of Lautrec, France, known for its faint taste of Dijon mustard, fiery Metechi from the Republic of Georgia, and the strong purple garlic of Las Pedroñeras, Spain, which has its own Designation of Origin. Garlics are divided into softnecks (best known for the easy-to-grow, braidable, long-storing California White varieties) and hardnecks (which include the more fragile and flavorful Porcelain, Purple Stripe, Marbled

---

[*] Botanists had used the lily family as a catch-all for plants that did not fit into other categories for years. In 2009, an international group of botanists removed three families including alliums from the lily group and grouped them in the amaryllis family.

Purple Stripe, Glazed Purple Stripe, Asiatic, Turban, and Creole varieties). Leave Elephant Garlic off the list. It's not really garlic; it's a leek.

The first thing you need to do is to choose what kind of garlic you want to plant based on your region and your taste buds. In the northern hemisphere, garlic is generally planted in the fall and harvested the following summer. Garlic requires forty days of vernalization (exposure to cold) for the cloves to sprout and develop bulbs. (It can be planted in the spring but the bulbs will not be as large so fall is really better.)

A lot of this information comes from well-known American garlic growers including the late Darrell Merrell (whose *Garlic Planting Guide* is used and recommended by Seed Savers Exchange in Decorah, Iowa), Bob Anderson of Gourmet Garlic Gardens, and Ted Jordan Meredith, author of *The Complete Book of Garlic*. I also consulted Natasha Edwards's wonderful book, *Garlic: The Mighty Bulb*. Edwards's father, Colin Boswell, is a passionate and enlightened alliophile and owner of The Garlic Farm on the Isle of Wight in the United Kingdom.

HOW TO PLANT GARLIC

Garlic can be planted from bulbils and from seed with limited (and mixed) results, as you'll read below. The easiest way to grow garlic plants is to separate and plant garlic cloves. For robust garlic, reserve the largest cloves for planting. The variety of cloves you choose to plant is the single greatest factor in determining your garlic-growing success. Each planted clove will yield one bulb.

BULBILS

The most economical way to grow garlic is to plant bulbils, the small bulbs that develop on a garlic scape if it's left on the plant and not cut off. Bulbils are essentially clones of the mother plant. These mini-bulbs will grow to be regular-sized bulbs although it may take several years. Bulbils can be planted closer together than regular bulbs as they will not grow to be as large. The size of mature cloves should be taken into account when spacing bulbils. Larger Rocambole bulbils should be planted four inches apart while Porcelains only need two inches between bulbils. The best choice for growing garlic from garlic bulbils are said to be Rocamboles and Asiatics followed by Purple Stripes.

GROWING GARLIC FROM SEED

While garlic has long been considered sterile, the idea of obtaining true seed from garlic goes back to 1875 when preeminent German botanist Eduard Regel found fertile wild garlic strains in Central Asia. Regel's discovery raised, for the first time, the possibility that some garlics in existence may still be capable of producing true seed.

The benefits of growing garlic from seed are to increase garlic's genetic diversity (making it more able to adapt to changing environmental conditions), improve its vitality and yield, and eliminate the viruses that are inherent in existing planting stock.

Ivan Buddenhagen, professor emeritus in the Department of Plant Sciences at UC Davis, started experimenting with obtaining true garlic seed fifteen years ago and now has ten different clones that he offers for sale at ivansnewgarlics.com. According to Buddenhagen, all of the garlics appear to be Rocamboles and have a "rich, well-rounded outstanding flavor." He reports success from growers in a variety of different climates including New York, Pennsylvania, Southern California, and Washington.

When to Plant

Garlic should be planted in the fall, between September 15 and November 30. Mid-October, just after the first light frost, is a good benchmark for most regions. Southern gardeners, who can plant later and harvest earlier, can plant as late as the end of December. Garlic can be planted in the late spring but, as mentioned earlier, the resultant bulbs will almost always be smaller.

The ancient tradition of planting according to the phases of the moon calls for garlic to be planted when the moon is waning. The amount of moonlight is decreasing and the gravitational pull is high so that moisture is pulled up in the soil (toward the moon). This is said to be good for root crops like garlic because the focus is on the part of the plant growing underground rather than the leaves growing above ground.

Where to Plant

Garlic grows best in rich, well-drained, organic soil that's free of weeds. Garlic is not a competitive plant; so good weed control is essential for healthy, vigorous bulbs. While garlic will tolerate shade, it thrives in full sun and likes soil with a pH between 6.5 and 7 (neutral to slightly acidic). Garlic is a light feeder, which means it depletes nutrients slowly and doesn't require a lot of fertilizer. Some soils benefit from additional nitrogen, but garlic doesn't need a lot of nitrogen, and if it gets too much, plants will grow vigorous leaves at the expense of small bulbs. To determine the needs of your soil, purchase an inexpensive soil test kit that will measure your soil's pH, nitrogen (N), phosphorous (P), and potassium (K); most kits also include a chart with optimal pH and N-P-K levels for different plants.

Planting the Garlic

While garlic's sulfuric compounds defend it against many adversaries, garlic is still susceptible to attack from diseases and pests. The most serious disease that affects garlic is white rot, which is caused by the fungus *Sclerotium cepivorum*. Once white rot infects an area, its spores can live in the soil for decades and garlic and other alliums should not be grown on the site. One way to reduce the incidence of disease and pest infestation is to rotate your garlic with other non-allium crops. If garlic is replanted in the same place year after year, there's an increased risk that allium diseases and pests will build up in the soil.

Opinions vary on whether or not garlic cloves need to be soaked before planting. Bob Anderson recommends soaking the separated cloves in a solution of one gallon of water, one tablespoon of baking soda, and one tablespoon of liquid seaweed for sixteen to twenty-four hours or until the clove covers loosen up and can be removed without harming the cloves. The clove covers might contain fungal spores or the eggs of pests, and baking soda neutralizes the fungi. Just before planting, soak the cloves in straight rubbing alcohol or 100-proof vodka for three or four minutes to kill any pathogens the first soak might have missed.

Another school of thought calls for planting unsoaked cloves with the clove skins intact so that the skins protect the cloves from infection. As the cloves shed their skins almost immediately, it's unlikely that the skins are critical, and while the double soaking might seem like overkill, it's a classic case of better safe than sorry. (Garlic pathogens don't usually manifest themselves until their damage has already been done so I think the extra step is worth it.)

In the meantime, prepare your garden bed for planting. Dig a furrow that's appropriate for your geographic region. Anderson recommends that garlic be planted two inches deep in the southern states, four inches deep in the northernmost states, and three inches deep in the rest of the country. Place the presoaked cloves into the furrow, spacing them six to eight inches apart. Garlic cloves should be planted root end down, pointed end up. The cloves should be planted two inches deep and six to eight inches apart. If you have planted several different varieties, draw a map so you will be able to identify the different types when you harvest them. After the cloves are in the ground, cover them with six inches of mulch. I like to mulch with shredded leaves, but you can use dried grass clippings, straw, compost, manure, or seaweed; don't use whole leaves as they are too heavy and could smother the garlic plants as well as the weeds. Don't remove the mulch in the spring as it will control weeds, retain moisture, and provide nutrients as it decomposes.

Garlic plants will emerge in early spring. Make sure the soil is not too dry; garlic needs about one inch of water per week during its spring growing season. Do not water plants after June 1 as they need to dry out in preparation for harvest and curing. You may want to spritz some fertilizer on the leaves of the plant once or twice during the growing season; this is called foliar feeding. Darrell Merrell's "prescription" is a gallon of water with a tablespoon each of fish emulsion and liquid seaweed added. Anderson recommends a blend of one gallon of water and a tablespoon each of fish emulsion, baking soda, and molasses.

Removing the Scapes

In early June, cut the scapes, the curly stems that hardneck garlics produce, after they reach about ten inches long. This will redirect the energy from the scape to the bulb. If scapes are allowed to keep growing, they will reduce the size of the bulb, sometimes by as much as 50 percent. The mildly garlicky scapes make a great pesto (recipe on page 132) and are a flavorful garnish in dips, pastas, soups, stir-fries, and anything else you can think of.

Harvest the Garlic

Harvest garlic when half to three-quarters of the leaves turn brown, typically in late June or early July. Dig each bulb out carefully and make sure not to break the stalk from the bulb as this can cause the bulb to rot. If you wait too long to harvest your garlic, the bulbs will begin in split in the ground.

Once your garlic is harvested, get it out of the sun and into a dry, shady, well-ventilated space as soon as possible. Tie the garlic together in bundles of six to ten bulbs and hang them to dry or "cure" for four to six weeks. Don't forget to label them if you've grown more than one variety, and if, unlike me, you didn't misplace your garlic planting map.

If you're planning to braid your softneck garlics, you can do this when they are half cured, after two or three weeks. When the bulbs are dry, trim off the roots and cut the stalks down to about half an inch to an inch. Garlic bulbs need to be able to breathe, so storing them in mesh bags or ventilated ceramic garlic keepers is optimal. I've also found those Asian bamboo steaming baskets that if, like me, you never use, are ideal, and the different levels let you store your different varieties separately. Don't store garlic in plastic bags or in the refrigerator as it will become soft and moldy.

Companion Planting

Companion planting is the practice of planting certain crops in proximity to each other to optimize pest control, pollination, and overall health. Thanks to its sulfuric compounds, garlic is beneficial to many different vegetables, fruits, flowers, and herbs—and it's detrimental to a few.

Garlic repels aphids, cabbage worms, slugs, and other pests, making it a beneficial companion to the following vegetables: lettuce, spinach, potatoes, eggplant, tomatoes, peppers, cabbage, broccoli, and kohlrabi. Garlic and beets are mutually beneficial to each other as both fend off leaf hoppers, worms, and flying pests. Don't plant garlic near beans, peas, or asparagus as it stunts their growth.

Garlic is a good companion to all fruit trees because its aroma repels aphids, caterpillars, mites, and Japanese beetles. (It can be planted at the base of the tree.) Garlic also attracts good insects by providing shelter, pollen, and nectar. More specifically, garlic protects peach trees from borers and apple trees from apple scab. It's also a good companion to flowers such as marigold, nasturtium, geranium, and petunias as it repels pests both above and below the ground. Garlic also deters deer and rabbits from eating these flowers. Roses and raspberries are beneficial to garlic for both growth and insect control. Garlic in turn assists roses by preventing disease and repelling aphids, ants, slugs, and other pests.

Garlic also complements and is complemented by herbs such as yarrow, summer savory, chamomile, rue, and dill. Yarrow and summer savory improve the overall health of garlic, and chamomile improves its flavor. Rue helps garlic by deterring maggots, while garlic helps dill by repelling spider mites. Garlic should not be planted near parsley or sage as it inhibits their growth.

The Genetics of Garlic

As early as the 1930s, leading German biologists were concerned with the preservation of plant varieties. Taking the knowledge of genetics as a starting point, research was conducted on cultivated plants using the methods and ideas developed in the fields of genetics, taxonomy, physiology, biochemistry, and biophysics with the goal of improving crop plant breeding.

The Kaiser Wilhelm Institute of Crop Plant Research was founded near Vienna in 1943. Hans Stubbe, its first head, began building up the institute in Gatersleben in 1945. After WWII, gene banks were established throughout the socialist European countries for the benefit of plant breeding.

The Gatersleben Gene Bank's existence was threatened by the reunification of Germany in 1990 and there was talk of closing it in favor of the inferior Crop Science and Seed Research Institute located in the West German city of Braunschweig. Fortunately, bureaucrats realized that crop collection and research facility was one of the few organizations that had been better run in former East Germany than in the West. (The West Germans focused on cereals and built a state-of-the-art gene bank in Ethiopia. Although they claimed that the project was "development cooperation," in reality, it was to preserve Ethiopian barley, essential for German beer.)

Dr. Joachim Keller of the Leibniz Institute of Plant Genetics and Crop Plant Research (as Gatersleben is now called) attributes the value of the Gatersleben's garlic collection to the high proportion of accessions directly collected in the various growing areas of Europe, the Mediterranean, and the garlic crescent area of Asia. Despite the hardship of life in the German Democratic Republic, the East German collectors never let up on the collection missions. And because of their alliance with the USSR, they were able to collect in Cuba, the Eastern Bloc, and North Korea—places that westerners would have had difficulty entering.

Today, Gatersleben remains a model for plant breeding and preservation, and Dr. Keller co-chairs the Allium Working Group for the European Cooperative Programme for Plant Genetic Resources. His work at Gatersleben is at the forefront of cryopreservation in which garlics are preserved in liquid nitrogen. Cryopreservation is superior to field cultivation because it protects the bulbs from infection and preserves their integrity by removing the influences of the field site. Because garlic does not form storable seeds and cloves have to be maintained for breeding and research, it's the ideal candidate for cryopreservation research and experimentation. Gatersleben propagates 1,140 allium species from around the world.

A GUIDE TO HEIRLOOM VARIETALS

Biologist Jeff Nekola, an advisor for Seed Savers Exchange, an organization devoted to saving and sharing heirloom seeds, grew and documented each of the garlic varieties in the Seed Savers collection, and his Heirloom Garlic Archive gives the backstories, both fascinating and mundane, of different varieties. For example, Russian Salvation was given to Helen Shultz's grandfather in gratitude for the refuge he gave to a Russian sailor who jumped ship in British Columbia; Mom's Oklahoma Rocambole was grown by Darrell Merrell's mother for twenty-five to thirty years in Tulsa; and Siberian garlic was obtained by fishermen bartering with peasant farmers. And Music isn't named for its beauty; it's named for Al Music, a Canadian garlic grower. This section highlights the different types of garlic, their histories, taste, and appearance characteristics. I've included a sampling of interesting, delicious, and available garlics.

Garlic is highly adaptable over time, but for success right out of the gate, it's wise to consider the garlic's country of origin. Siberian garlic from the frozen tundra of Russia is well suited to icy northern winters; Creole garlics from Spain and Artichoke garlics like Sicilian Gold are better suited to milder climates.

Hardnecks (*Allium sativum ophioscorodon*)

Hardneck garlics are characterized by a woody central stalk that's surrounded by a single circle of cloves. The stalk or scape is succulent in early spring and should be cut off to make sure the energy is directed from the stalk to the bulb. The scape is sometimes called a false seed head because no fertile seed is produced. If the scape is left on, it will form an umbel, a capsule on top of the flower stalk that encloses small aerial cloves known as bulbils. Bulbils can be planted and will eventually turn into bulbs, but it may take several years and the bulbils will have to be harvested and replanted every year until they achieve a normal bulb size. Hardneck garlic is also known as top-setting garlic and serpent garlic.

Rocamboles

Rocamboles are the most widely known and planted hardnecks. They have a more full-bodied flavor than softnecks and are sweeter and less sulfurous than other garlic groups. (If you like raw garlic, zesty Rocamboles are your top choice.) Rocamboles produce large cloves that are easily peeled, making them popular with chefs. They have a shorter storage life than most other varieties because of their loose outer skins. Because Rocamboles thrive in cold winter climates with rich loamy soil and need a period of vernalization, they are considered a northern garlic and are not a good choice for warm southern climates. Bulb wrappers are a dull brownish tan. Rocamboles grow thick, tightly coiled scapes that should be removed so the plant focuses its growing energy on the bulb. Most strains average six to eleven cloves per bulb in a single circle around the stem and have an average shelf life of five to six months.

Carpathian This garlic from the Carpathian Mountains of southwest Poland has large, uniform bulbs with few double cloves. It has classic garlic flavor, nice overall tang, and typical Rocambole hotness and spiciness. Carpathian was selected as one of *Cook's Illustrated*'s favorite varieties.

German Red This rich, strong, and very spicy garlic came to this country (to Idaho) over a hundred years ago with German immigrants and continues to flourish in colder regions. A vigorous grower with purple and brown skin, this variety is one of the hottest-tasting Rocamboles when raw. Double cloves are common.

Killarney Red An outstanding Rocambole named for Killarney Farm in Idaho, this garlic's original source is unknown but it may be derived from German Red or Spanish Roja. This variety adapts better to wet conditions than most Rocamboles, making it well suited to the Pacific Northwest. It has a typical spicy Rocambole flavor with a lingering finish.

Russian Red This cultivar was introduced to the United States via Canada by Russian Doukhobor immigrants in the late 1800s. (The Doukhobors were a pacifistic religious sect whose migration from Russia was financed primarily by Quakers and Leo Tolstoy.) Russian Red is known for its strong, musky flavor and pleasing sweet aftertaste. It's very hot when eaten raw.

Spanish Roja A northwestern heirloom with century-old roots in the Portland, Oregon, area, this rich, robust garlic is a favorite of many northwestern garlic growers who think it has the perfect flavor of true garlic. Some growers credit Spanish Roja with sparking the renaissance of garlic growing among small farmers.

Temptress Introduced by the Garlic Seed Foundation in upstate New York (a nonprofit organization that provides seed stock and garlic-growing information), Temptress has a sharp initial taste that mellows over time. It thrives in cold weather.

Porcelains

Porcelains are becoming increasingly popular as both gardeners and garlic connoisseurs discover these beautiful, flavorful bulbs. They grow very tall, sometimes as high as seven feet. Their outstanding flavor rivals that of Rocamboles, and thanks to their smooth, tight bulb wrappers, they can be stored longer. As with other hardnecks, Porcelain garlics produce beautiful curling scapes that must be cut to redirect the energy to the bulb. (According to Ted Jordon Meredith, Porcelains are more sensitive to this than other varieties and he cautions that "leaving the scapes untrimmed is an invitation to highly diminished bulbs at harvest.") Porcelain garlics are also known for having higher levels of allicin than other types. Although the bulbs are typically very large, they usually have only four to six cloves and an average shelf life of eight months.

Georgian Fire My personal favorite, this white-hot porcelain garlic from the Republic of Georgia was one of many rescued from obscurity by the Gatersleben Gene Bank. Like its mellower sibling, Georgian Crystal, it comes from the mountainous Cichisdzhvari, an agricultural region located between the Black and Caspian Seas. (It's also known by its tongue-twisting sobriquet, Cichisdzhvari #4. Georgian Crystal is Cichisdzhvari #1. I don't know what happened to Cichisdzhvaris #2 and #3). Georgian Fire has beautiful, papery white skins and, as advertised, a hot, fiery flavor.

Georgian Crystal This mellow, fresh-tasting garlic is known for bulbs so big and beautiful that they're sometimes mistaken for Elephant Garlic. Georgian Crystal lacks the heat that characterizes most of its fellow Porcelains and is a good all-around garlic. Thanks to its pure garlic flavor and large, easy-to-peel cloves, it's popular with chefs and restaurants. As it grows well everywhere and needs very little attention, Georgian Crystal is a great starter garlic.

German Extra Hardy Also known as German White, this garlic has very long roots that make it one of the most winter-friendly garlics. It produces very large bulbs each with four or five large cloves. Its external skin is white and the skin covering the cloves is dark red. German Extra Hardy has a strong, raw flavor and a high sugar content, making it one on the best garlics for roasting.

Erik's German White Grown by Erik Sessions at Patchwork Green Farm in Decorah, Iowa, it is one of two garlic varieties grown in President Obama's White House garden. Like German Extra Hardy, bulbs have white wrappers with reddish-purple, easy-to-peel cloves and a rich, spicy garlic flavor. (The other variety grown in the White House garden is Samarkand, a Purple Stripe.)

Leningrad Despite its name, this cultivar is originally from Belarus. While Leningrad can grow anywhere, it thrives in regions with cold winters and is not ideal for hot southern climates. It's also immune to a lot of the diseases that plague garlic. Leningrad's flavor starts out sweet and mild but crescendos for a full minute to a sharp, lingering heat. (This is an "I'll have what she's having" garlic.)

Romanian Red This variety came to British Columbia via Romania and might be one of the earliest Porcelain garlics grown in the Americas. Romanian Red has the highest level of allicin of any known garlic. The high allicin content gives it a hot, sulfurous flavor. The giant, easy-to-peel cloves make this a perennial chef's favorite. It's also one of the most disease-resistant varieties.

Rosewood This garlic is from Moldova (my father's ancestral homeland), so I'm especially pleased to see it catching on. Rosewood is a relatively small garlic with four nice-sized cloves. It's robust with a bold, lingering aftertaste. An added bonus: Rosewood can be stored for up to ten months.

Purple Stripes

Named for the bright purple streaks and dapples on both its bulb wrappers and clove skins, Purple Stripes—and its junior siblings, Glazed Purple Stripes and Marbled Purple Stripes—are the stunning supermodels of the garlic world. These garlics are most genetically similar to original garlic, and all other garlic varieties are, in a sense, descended from Purple Stripes. Purple Stripes are very flavorful and frequently win "best baked garlic" in nationwide taste tests. They are easy to grow and store slightly longer than Rocamboles. They peel relatively easily (but not as easily as Rocamboles), and while they can be grown in poor quality soil, they will thrive and reward you with big beautiful bulbs when grown in rich soil. Most Purple Stripes have eight to twelve cloves per bulb and an average shelf life of five to six months.

Belarus Collected from Belarus during Soviet times, the aptly named Belarus is a hearty, medium-bodied garlic with a rich, lingering flavor. It's excellent roasted but does not store as well as other Purple Stripes. Belarus is one of the favorite garlics of Dr. Richard Hannan who was the curator of the USDA's garlic collection (and would know a thing or two about great garlic!).

Chesnok Red Originally called Shvelisi after the village it came from, Chesnok Red is another Georgian gem. This full-flavored garlic is a great cooking garlic because it's easy to peel and retains its shape and flavor after cooking. It's creamy and sweet when roasted. It's a late-harvesting garlic that growers love because the cloves are the same size. (You always want to reserve the largest cloves for planting, so with some garlics, that means you're stuck with lots of tiny clove slivers when you put aside the larger ones.)

Samarkand Although it was found by John Swenson at a market in Uzbekistan, this garlic was known as Persian Star for several years because garlic grower Horace Shaw thought "it sounded Persian." The name stuck for a few years but it's now been rightfully christened Samarkand. Samarkand is full-flavored but packs less heat than many Purple Stripes. With its thick white bulb wrappers that reveal purple streaks as you peel them away, it's one of the most beautiful of the Purple Stripes. When the wrappers are all peeled away the clove covers with their distinctive long sharp points resemble an eight-point star, hence the name.

Glazed Purple Stripes

Both Glazed Purple Stripes and Marbled Purple Stripes used to be classified as a subgroup of Purple Stripes but are now considered distinct cultivars. Both Glazed and Marbled have fewer, fatter cloves than standard Purple Stripes. Glazed Purple Stripes are not commonly grown because they have delicate wrappers that require careful handling and timely harvesting. Their shiny wrappers look metallic and depending on growing conditions may have gold or silver overtones. They have nine to twelve cloves per bulb and an average shelf life of five months.

Purple Glazer Also known as Mchadidzhvari #1 after its Georgian home, this garlic is a real head turner. While the outer wrappers are satiny white, in the right growing conditions, the inner wrappers are striking, solid purple tinged with silver. The flavor is mild, making it a lovely, not too strong raw garlic. Purple Glazers become sweet when roasted.

Red Rezan This variety was collected in Rezan (more accurately transliterated as Ryazan), a central Russian city southeast of Moscow. It has a nice garlicky flavor without heat or a lingering aftertaste. It thrives in a very cold climate.

Marbled Purple Stripes

Along with Creole garlic, Marbled Purple Stripes are one of the best kinds of garlic for growing in hot climates, although unlike Creoles, they also grow well in cold regions. They are heartier than Glazed Purple Stripes and therefore increasingly valued by commercial growers.

Marbled Purple Stripes have brown dappling (or marbling) on the outer wrappers and cloves. They have five to nine cloves and an average shelf life of six months.

Bogatyr This very large Moscow-born garlic came to the United States from Gatersleben. This is a garlic-fan favorite with a lot of heat up front followed by a pleasant lingering aftertaste. Bogatyr is the longest storing of the Marbled Purple Stripes and can last up to ten months.

Choparsky Collected from the Siberian Botanical Garden in Khabarovsk, a city in far eastern Russia that borders China, Choparsky is hot when raw but mellows nicely when cooked. It has large cloves, making it useful in recipes calling for a lot of garlic.

Kitab John Swenson and the USDA team found this garlic in a dry riverbed in the mountains of Uzbekistan. The bulbs were buried so deeply that no one could extract them, so the group was limited to the handfuls of bulbils that they brought back and grew into bulbs. Kitab has a strong, straightforward garlic taste without the complexity of other Purple Stripes.

Krasnodar Red This Marbled Purple Stripe by Krasnodar, Russia, near the Black Sea was brought to this country by Dr. Carl Rosen, a soil scientist at the University of Minnesota. It used to be hard to find but is increasingly available at garlic festivals and online. It has a strong but not too spicy flavor when raw and holds its flavor well when cooked.

Metechi This blush-skinned garlic produces large, fat cloves that are very hot when raw. Although it hails from Georgia and thrives in cold winters, it's also one of the most reliable hardneck garlics for areas with warm winters. Metechi is a late season, long-storing garlic.

Pskem Originally collected from the Pskem River Valley in Uzbekistan by John Swenson on the 1989 garlic-collecting mission, this garlic has a rich, spicy flavor with a lingering aftertaste. It has between two and four large cloves.

Siberian This cold-friendly variety hails from the frozen tundra of Siberia's Kamchatka Peninsula where it was obtained by fishermen bartering with peasant farmers. A pink-skinned garlic (that reddens in iron-rich soil), Siberian garlic has a medium to strong flavor and a high allicin content.

Asiatics

Asiatic garlics, as well as Turban garlics (see below), were classified as Artichoke garlics until DNA research conducted by Dr. Gayle Volk of the USDA and Dr. Joachim Keller of the Leibniz Institute for Plant Genetics and Crop Plant Research in Gatersleben showed them both to be weakly bolting hardnecks that are distinct from each other as well as from the other groups of garlics. Asiatic bulbs have firm, plump cloves with thick, glossy wrappers. Bulbs have a tendency to be pure white, but cloves may be richly colored in purple or mahogany. Asiatic garlics mature very suddenly, just ahead of Artichokes. They should be harvested just as soon as leaves begin to brown. If you wait until almost half of the leaves are brown you may find that the bulb wrappers have already split open. Unlike other hardnecks, you don't need to remove the scapes (which are less pronounced than other scapes and may not even appear at all in warm climates) to be assured of large bulbs. They tend to have eight to twelve cloves and an average shelf life of five months.

Asian Tempest (aka Seoul Sister) This South Korean garlic is hot when raw, and sweet and flavorful when cooked. It's a long-storing garlic that grows well in regions with both cold and wet, mild winters. Asian Tempest is sweet when roasted.

Korean Red This tan-and-pink-colored garlic has beautiful pure garlic flavor without any heat. It's a kinder, gentler garlic for those who enjoy rich garlic taste without the risk of fire. An early season garlic, Korean

Red's zesty flavor makes it, not surprisingly, good for kimchi and stir-fries.

Pyongyang From near the capital of North Korea, this garlic has light brown cloves with a purplish blush and elongated tips. It has a light, mild flavor with a slight bit of heat when eaten raw. Pyongyang can be stored longer than most other Asiatics.

Turbans

Turbans, weakly bolting garlics like Asiatics, are often striped with purple and have, on average, six tan or pinkish cloves. Cloves tend to be thinner than those of other garlics. Like Asiatic garlics, Turbans are harvested early but cannot be stored for long periods. Turban garlics are named for the turban-shaped *umbels* (seed pods) that form on the end of their scapes. They tend to have six large cloves and an average shelf life of five months.

Blossom This garlic has large, white bulbs with dark purplish stripes. It's hot when raw but mellows nicely when roasted. Blossom was brought to the United States by Greg Czarnecki who purchased it at the Hongqiao (Pearl) Market near the Temple of Heaven in Beijing.

China Dawn This purple-lined bulb has a rich garlic taste with a sweet, almost floral aftertaste. It has a slight bite on the finish. China Dawn is an early harvesting garlic (late spring or early summer).

Shilla Hailing from Korea, Shilla is a beautiful garlic with purple striping and a deep, rich flavor with a moderately pungent finish. As an early harvesting garlic, it should be one of the first garlics planted in the fall.

Xian Chester Aaron, a former college professor who became a prolific garlic farmer and wrote the charming garlic memoir *Garlic Is Life*, paid thirty dollars for a single bulb of this garlic that a worker at the Green Lotus restaurant in San Francisco's Chinatown had smuggled in from Xian, China in 1995. It remained one of Aaron's favorite varieties.

Softnecks (*Allium sativum sativum*)

Softneck garlics have a soft central stem surrounded by several layers of cloves. They are non-bolting, which means they don't produce scapes or flowers. They're easy to grow and thrive in varying soils and climates. Softnecks produce large bulbs and make lovely braids. These garlics are especially long lasting and when stored properly can last up to ten months. They tend to be either very mild or very hot (and cold winters produce hotter bulbs).

Artichokes

Artichoke strains are very vigorous and large bulbed; they are the easiest variety to grow and grow well in warm climates. The most common Artichoke varieties are California Early and California Late, the varieties grown by Christopher Ranch in Gilroy. (Christopher Ranch is responsible for most of the garlic grown in the United States.) Artichokes are named for their configuration of several overlapping layers of cloves, reminiscent of an actual artichoke. Many Artichoke strains have three to five clove layers containing twelve to twenty total cloves and an average shelf life of seven to eight months.

California Early California Early and California Late are the juggernauts of the commercial garlic-growing industry, and it's easy to see why. California Early adapts well to a variety of climates, matures early (as its name suggests), and stores well. Most bulbs have four layers of cloves and ten to fourteen cloves per bulb. The bulbs can be huge and the inner cloves are not annoyingly small as they can be in other varieties. The mild flavor makes it suitable for a wide range of tastes. As bacon is frequently the gateway meat for former vegetarians, California Early is a gateway garlic.

~~ Nikolai Vavilov, Seed Saving, and Crop Diversity

Nikolai Vavilov, the great Russian botanist, identified Central Asia as the birthplace of garlic. Vavilov, who roamed the earth collecting and preserving seeds, was the foremost crop geneticist and plant geographer of his time (1887–1943). He conducted over one hundred collecting missions to sixty-four countries in addition to his missions within Russia. During his distinguished career he formed and led the All-Union Institute of Applied Botany, which became the world's largest crop research institute. He built the institute's seed collections by scouring five continents in the 1920s and 1930s for wild and cultivated corn, potato tubers, grains, beans, fodder, seeds, and garlic. Tragically, he fell afoul of Stalin and died of malnutrition in a prison camp. Four of his disciples died of starvation at their desks rather than break into his storied collection. The people on the garlic-collecting mission of 1989 kicked off their trip with a symbolic and poignant visit to Vavilov's office in St. Petersburg.

Vavilov is especially relevant today because crop diversity and seed preservation are very hot topics. Scientists fear that the world's crop diversity is threatened by both actual events (global warming and the globalization of agribusiness) and potential ones (nuclear and biological warfare, political upheaval, and land mismanagement). Without diversity, the global food supply is more susceptible to pests and disease. The Bill and Melinda Gates Foundation has invested $30 million in the Svalbard Global Seed Vault (better known as the Doomsday Vault), an iron-clad safe house for preserving seeds that's built into a mountain on a remote Norwegian island near the Arctic Ocean.

Although the twentieth century was generally viewed as catastrophic for crop diversity, garlic was one of the century's big diversity winners (along with tomatoes, squash, lettuce, beans, and peppers). There were three garlic varieties available in 1903; in 2004, there were a staggering 274 thanks to collectors, preservationists, importers, and breeders.

California Late California Late is smaller (though not small), hotter, stores better, and grows better in warm climates than its Early sibling. It's nice when roasted and generally inoffensive. If you prefer braiding your garlic to eating it, this is the garlic for you.

Inchelium Red One of the most productive of all the heirloom garlics, this softneck variety was discovered on the Colville Indian Reservation in Inchelium, Washington, and is believed to be one of the oldest garlic strains grown in the Americas. Inchelium Red is sweeter and milder than other varieties and has consistently won high marks (often taking first place) in garlic tastings. On the plus side, it adapts to both mild and cold climates and stores incredibly well. On the negative side, its mild flavor might disappoint lovers of hot, pungent garlics. Slow Food USA has recognized Inchelium Red and Lorz Italian (below) as Arc of Taste products, a collection of over 200 delicious foods deemed in danger of extinction.

Lorz Italian An old heirloom variety that the Lorz family brought from their native Italy to Washington State's Columbia River Basin in the early 1900s, Lorz Italian is a strong, richly flavored garlic. It can become quite spicy if grown during hot summers. One bulb can have anywhere from two to eighteen cloves.

Simoneti Despite its Italian-sounding name, this garlic was collected by Philipp Simon in the Georgian village of Simoneti on the banks of the Black Sea. It's one of the mildest of the Artichoke varieties. While it thrives and produces extra-large bulbs in rich soil, it's one of the few Artichokes that can also be grown in poor soil.

Polish White Also known as New York White, this is one of the most cold-tolerant Artichoke varieties and is especially productive in the northeast. It produces large cloves with few or no small, slivery inner cloves. It has a rich, deep flavor with very little bite. While it's great for eating and cooking, Polish White is also great for braiding thanks to its satiny white parchment wrappings tinted with purple.

Red Toch Also known as Tochliavri after the Georgian village where it was found, Red Toch thrives in both cold and warm climates. With its mild but flavorful taste, Red Toch is a favorite of the late Tulsa garlic grower Darrell Merrell and his friend, Chester Aaron. (Aaron's father was born in the village of Tochliavri). This garlic has a subtle flavor when roasted.

Susanville This flavorful garlic is considered an improved strain of California Early. Although originally from California, it also does well in colder climates. Like its progenitor, Susanville has large, easy-to-peel cloves and is a long-storing variety.

Thermadrone This large, long-storing garlic hails from the Drôme region in southeast France where it's grown commercially and called Thermidrome. Somehow when it arrived in the United States, it acquired the ridiculous, military-sounding name: Thermadrone. Whatever it's called, this full-flavored garlic has a lovely Dijon mustard overtone that makes it a natural for French dishes.

Silverskins

Silverskin garlics are popular with commercial growers as they are the highest-yielding variety, grow well in a wide range of climates, and have a very long storage life. They range in taste from mild to spicy. They're also the most popular garlics for braiding because of the smooth, shiny skin and symmetrical shape. These are the last garlics harvested in the season (July to August). Silverskins usually have three clove layers with twelve to twenty cloves per bulb and an average shelf life of ten months or longer.

Nootka Rose From Nootka Rose Farm in Washington's San Juan Islands, this beautiful bulb has silky-smooth skins with some pink blush on its outer cloves. The inside cloves are an exotic mahogany color. Nootka Rose garlic makes beautiful braids. This is a late-maturing garlic with a nice strong flavor and anywhere from eight to twenty cloves. It's average storage time is eleven months.

Rose du Var Originally from the heart of Provence, this pink-tinged garlic is known for its hot, pungent taste. It features an attractive bulb and cloves with nice reddish colors. There are several layers of cloves but no slivers.

S&H Silverskin Originally from S&H Organic Acres in Oregon's Willamette wine region, this rich-tasting garlic has a mild aftertaste. The longer it's stored, however, the hotter it is when eaten raw. Unlike many Silverskin garlics, S&H Silverskins have very few tiny cloves.

Silverwhite Silverwhites are creamy-white beautiful bulbs filled with dark burgundy-colored cloves. They have a rich, deep garlic flavor and taste mild initially, but give it fifteen seconds and the taste crescendos to a long-lasting surge of fiery heat.

Creoles

Once thought to be a Silverskin garlic, Creoles are now recognized as a unique cultivar. These garlics have bright-white wrappers and brilliant clove colors ranging from rosy pink to deep purple. Initially cultivated in Spain, they were spread throughout Europe by the conquistadores and brought to the United States by Spanish explorers. They tend to be sweet tasting and are a long-storing variety. As befitting their name,

Creoles perform best in southern locations and places with mild winter climates as they require a long and sunny growing season to thrive. When eaten raw, they have a full taste that's warm but not too hot. An important thing to know about Creole garlics is that the cloves don't develop until the last minute so gardeners are cautioned not to pick them too soon. Creoles shouldn't be picked until the stalks are almost completely dead and withered. They have anywhere between five and nine cloves and an average shelf life of nine to ten months.

Ajo Rojo Ajo Rojo's white wrappers open to reveal stunning rose-colored cloves with red, purple, and maroon streaks. Ajo Rojo has an initial sweet bite that increases in its intensity; its aftertaste is warm, rather than hot.

Burgundy Less pungent than Ajo Rojo, Burgundy has a sweet, mellow flavor with a mildly spicy aftertaste. Its deep-rose wrappers contain the stunning Burgundy wine–colored cloves that give it its name. While most Creole garlics have elongated cloves, Burgundy's cloves are round and squat.

Creole Red This crowd pleaser was a top vote getter when garlic grower and author Chester Aaron conducted over fifty garlic tastings around the country during the release of his "garlic memoir," *Garlic is Life*. Unfortunately for northern growers, Creole Red grows much better in warm, southern climates.

Cuban Purple This Creole from Spain was originally called Rojo de Castro after Fidel until, I'm guessing, someone in marketing decided that Communist dictators didn't make for great branding. It's now known as Cuban Purple—and with its sweet, mild but full flavor, it's a great raw addition to salsa that will appeal to a wide range of tastes. While all Creoles are well suited to warm climates, according to Meredith, Cuban Purple thrives especially well in very hot weather.

⌇ Garlic Festivals around the World

Gilroy Garlic Festival
5,000 tickets were printed for the first Gilroy Garlic Festival. When 15,000 people turned up, volunteers had to sell the tickets, collect them, and rush them back to the admissions booth so they could be sold again. It was 1979. Garlic was still mildly subversive and decidedly lower-class.

A few years ago, I joined the revelers at Gilroy's folksy, fun, and family-friendly festival. I tasted garlic ice cream, something that was, to borrow from author David Foster Wallace, a supposedly fun thing I'll never do again. I savored Gilroy Garlic Fries and relished a platter of Garlic Scampi cooked up by the festival's Pyro Chefs in Gourmet Alley. The Pyro Chefs are famous for their spectacular grill flame-ups—which send fiery flames rocketing five feet in the air.

I watched the finals of the recipe contest cook-off in which the winning recipe was a sweet surprise: Spicy Garlic Butter Cookies with Garlic Goat Cheese and Honey. Winner Andrew Barth donned the coveted garlic crown and pocketed $1,000. I learned how to braid garlic, and I walked away with a Gilroy Garlic Festival apron that I won because I was the only person in the stadium during the cook-off who knew that the end of the Indian proverb, "Garlic is as good as . . ." was "ten mothers," not "sex," "chocolate," or "anything else."

Hudson Valley Garlic Festival
The country's second-largest garlic festival is the Hudson Valley Garlic Festival in Saugerties, New York. The New York festival features a wide array of garlic varieties, unlike Gilroy, which

continued

spotlights only California White. Because of all the farmers and the different varieties, it's my favorite garlic festival in the world. My first year, I went to the second day of the festival, but now I make sure to go on the first day—because on the second day, I was told that some of the exhibitors were a bit hungover from their first-night get-together.

Freud, not a big fan of American culture, would have hated the festival. The father of psychoanalysis once told a patient, "You Americans are like this. Garlic's good. Chocolate's good. Let's put a little garlic on chocolate and eat it." A Hudson Valley festival favorite is local chocolatier Oliver Kita's luscious Garlic Truffles. Kita also whips up Roasted Garlic Caramels for Halloween.

The Rose Garlic Festival in Lautrec, France

Lautrec is a small, beautiful village in France that's famous for its delicate rose garlic. It holds an annual garlic festival on the first Friday in August. Somewhat poetically, you park on a harvested garlic field. The event kicks off with a parade by the Brotherhood of the Garlic, whose members are clad in medieval-style robes and carry a flag standard. They are accompanied by brotherhoods of everything from Bordeaux wine to carrots. The highlight of the festival is the free garlic soup (accompanied by free rosé wine). The soup looks like water after you've cleaned white paint off a paintbrush but don't let that deter you. It's fabulous, with soft garlic flavor in a light broth with vermicelli (recipe on page 148).

Takko-Machi, Japan

The city of Takko-Machi, Japan's largest garlic producer, throws a Beef and Garlic Festival every October. Since it's located near the United States' Misawa Air Base, the festival features American country music, dancing, and Texas BBQ "Japanese style." Takko-Machi is a sister city of Gilroy, California, and each year, the

Gilroy Garlic Queen and her court attend the festival. In return, Takko-Machi always sends a delegation to the Gilroy festival and junior high and high school students take an annual school field trip to Gilroy. Takko-Machi also has a garlic center that features the Gilroy Cafe, a fusion restaurant where menu items range from garlic ramen to garlic ice cream.

Japanese garlic restaurants have spread throughout the country and to our shores. Like the Gilroy Cafe, Garlic Jo's also pays homage to Gilroy; its outlets are decorated to resemble "an old-fashioned Gilroy farmhouse . . . where we can feel the warmth from the vast garlic field." Garlic Jo's has recently expanded to the United States and has an outpost in Newport Beach for those Northern Californians homesick for Gilroy. Another chain, Ninniku-Ya (a Japanese variant of *garlic*), serves garlicky food from around the world (escargot, filet mignon, four-mushroom pasta, and garlic gelato) at its outposts in Tokyo, Hokkaido, and Honolulu, Hawaii. And in Okinawa, Arin Krin (The Garlic House) goes over the top with deep-fried garlic topped with garlic aioli.

Part Two

RECIPES

Recipe List

GARLIC HANDLING
AND PREPARATION

The recipes in this book call for garlic in a number of different forms: whole heads, cloves, peeled and unpeeled, crushed, minced, mashed to a paste, sliced, and roasted.

HOW MUCH GARLIC?

Some recipes call for whole heads of garlic, some call for a specific number of cloves, and still others call for a measured amount like tablespoons or cups. Here are some general tips about how much garlic to use:

    1 average head = 8 to 10 cloves
    1 garlic clove = 1 teaspoon minced garlic
    1 cup garlic cloves = 6 ounces garlic

SEPARATING A HEAD OF GARLIC INTO CLOVES

Wrap the head in a cloth and then put the garlic on a work surface. Press down on the garlic firmly, rolling it as you press down. The skin will break, and the head will separate into cloves.

TO PEEL GARLIC

If you are planning to mince or mash garlic, the easiest way to peel it is with the flat side of a chef's knife. Lay the blade on top of the clove, and hit the blade firmly with the side of your fist.

If you want to leave the garlic clove as intact as possible, use a paring knife to trim away the end of the clove and then pull the skin away.

TO MINCE GARLIC

Chop the garlic with a very sharp knife as follows: Hold the tip of the blade in place with one hand to make a fulcrum. Chop the blade up and down, periodically scraping the garlic from the side of the knife and back into the pile.

Another option, if you need to mince a lot of garlic, is to use a food processor or blender.

TO MASH GARLIC TO A PASTE

This technique takes minced garlic one step further. Mince the garlic as described above. When it is evenly minced, sprinkle the garlic with some salt. Hold the blade of the knife almost parallel to your work surface, and scrape the garlic back and forth over the work surface with the edge of the blade until it is mashed to a fine puree.

TO ROAST GARLIC

Preheat the oven to 325°F. Cut a piece of aluminum foil large enough to wrap around the garlic head. Cut off the top ¼ inch of the garlic head. Set the garlic, cut side up, in the center of the foil. Drizzle the exposed cloves with olive oil. Pull the corners of the foil in to the center, make a pouch around the garlic, and twist the top to secure the pouch closed. Place the foil pouch in a small baking dish or pan. Roast the garlic until the cloves are soft and any juices are brown, about 45 minutes.

TO PUREE ROASTED GARLIC

When the garlic is cool enough to handle but still warm, squeeze the cloves out of the papery skin and into a bowl; mash the roasted garlic with a fork into a smooth puree.

Garlic can be roasted and pureed up to 2 days in advance. Place the puree in a container, and top it with a little oil. Cover the container, and keep it in the refrigerator.

DIPS, SAUCES, AND CONDIMENTS

Roasted Garlic Hummus
(Lebanese Chickpea Dip)

This chickpea dip, claimed by Lebanon, is made with an entire head of roasted garlic. Try topping it with za'atar, a Middle Eastern blend of dried herbs, sesame seeds, and salt.

MAKES 2 CUPS

2 cups chickpeas, cooked or canned, rinsed and drained

1 head garlic, roasted and pureed

¼ cup warm water

2 tbsp tahini

1 lemon, juiced

¼ tsp kosher salt

¼ cup extra-virgin olive oil, to serve

Chopped parsley, for garnish

Paprika, for garnish

Za'atar, for garnish

1. Combine the chickpeas, garlic, warm water, tahini, lemon juice, and salt in a food processor. Puree until the mixture is smooth and light. Adjust the consistency by adding either a little water or lemon juice. The hummus can be stored at this point in a covered container in the refrigerator for up to 3 days.

2. To serve: Allow the hummus to come to room temperature. Spoon it into a bowl, drizzle it with olive oil, and sprinkled it with parsley, paprika, and/or za'atar. Accompany the hummus with crudités, pita or other flatbreads, or crackers.

....

Skordalia
(Greek Potato and Garlic Dip)

Skordalia is made up of the Greek and Italian words for garlic, so the name means essentially "garlicky garlic." Potatoes might be replaced with soaked stale bread in some traditional versions (or simply omitted in others), but whatever the base, this dip is really all about the garlic, the olive oil, and the lemon juice. It is popular throughout Greece as a sauce served with fried fish, on its own (with or without a salad of wild greens), or simply slathered on bread or crackers. Use a large wooden bowl, if you have one, to mix the skordalia. The wood surface helps to puree the potatoes for a light, smooth texture.

MAKES 2 CUPS

2 large russet potatoes, peeled, cut into small cubes
1 tsp kosher salt, divided
6 garlic cloves
1 large egg yolk
¾ cup extra-virgin olive oil, divided, plus more if needed
¼ cup fresh lemon juice
3 tbsp white wine vinegar
Freshly ground black pepper, to taste

1. Put the potatoes in a pot and add enough cold water to cover them by at least 1 inch. Add ½ teaspoon of the salt. Bring the water to a simmer over medium heat and cook the potatoes until they are tender enough to mash easily, 10 to 12 minutes. Drain them well in a colander.

2. Pound the garlic and the remaining salt in a large bowl (wooden if available) with a pestle until the garlic is thoroughly mashed. Gradually add the hot potatoes, pounding them into the garlic until the mixture is smooth before each subsequent addition.

3. Add the egg yolk and beat it in with the pestle or a wooden spoon. Add about ¼ cup of the olive oil and continue to beat until the mixture is smooth. Add the lemon juice and blend well. Add another ¼ cup of the oil, followed by the white wine vinegar, and ending with the final ¼ cup of the oil. Blend the mixture between each addition until it is smooth.

4. Mix in more olive oil, or some water, a little at a time, if the sauce is too thick to use as a dip. Season the dip with pepper to taste. Skordalia can be prepared up to 2 days in advance. Place the dip in a container, cover it tightly, and keep it in the refrigerator. Let the skordalia return to room temperature and check the consistency and seasoning before serving.

5. Serve the dip directly from the mixing bowl or transfer it to another serving bowl. Accompany it with crudités, pita crisps, bagel chips, or crackers.

....

Acii Esme
(Turkish Yogurt Sauce)

This sauce has a great flavor and texture when made in a mortar and pestle, as in this recipe. But there is nothing wrong with simply mashing the garlic into a paste using a knife (page 122) and then stirring the ingredients together.

4 garlic cloves, peeled
1 tsp kosher salt
1 cup Greek yogurt
½ tsp Harissa, or more to taste (see below)
Extra-virgin olive oil, to serve

1. Pound the garlic and salt together in a mortar with a pestle until the garlic is thoroughly mashed.
2. Add the yogurt and harissa to the mortar and blend the mixture with the pestle until it is thoroughly combined. This sauce can be prepared up to 1 day in advance. Place the sauce in a container, cover it tightly, and keep it in the refrigerator.
3. Serve the sauce directly from the mortar or transfer it to a serving bowl. Just before serving, drizzle olive oil on top of the acii esme.
4. Accompany the sauce with crudités, pita, or similar flatbreads, or serve it as an accompaniment to kebabs or grilled meats, fried vegetables, or savory fritters.

Harissa
(Hot Chili Paste)

Harissa is used in the North African cuisines of Morocco, Tunisia, and Algeria. It can be added to vinaigrettes, soups, pasta, grain dishes, sandwiches, and marinades for fish, meat, and poultry.

MAKES I CUP

6 oz dried red chilies (such as cayenne or chile de arbol)
12 garlic cloves, peeled
1 tbsp ground coriander
1 tbsp ground cumin
1 tbsp ground caraway seeds
1 tbsp salt

½ cup chopped cilantro

½ cup extra-virgin olive oil, plus more to store

1. Combine the chilies, garlic, coriander, cumin, caraway, and salt in a food processor, and pulse the machine on and off until the mixture is a coarse paste.
2. Add the cilantro to the food processor, close the lid, and with the processor, running, pour the oil in a thin stream through the feed tube. Continue to process just until you have a fine, smooth paste.
3. Harissa lasts for 2 weeks (or more). Place it in a jar and cover it with a layer of oil. Close the jar tightly and store it in the refrigerator. Replace the layer of oil each time you use some.

....

Aioli

Serve this classic French sauce with poached or grilled fish, as a dressing, stirred into soups or stews, or as a sandwich spread.

MAKES I CUP

1 large egg yolk, room temperature

3 garlic cloves, minced

Kosher salt, to taste

¾ cup extra-virgin olive oil

2 tsp lemon juice, plus more as needed

Freshly ground black pepper, to taste

1. To make the aioli by hand: Put the egg yolk in a medium bowl. Add the garlic and a pinch of salt and whisk to combine them. While whisking, add the olive oil a few drops at a time, until half of the oil is blended into the egg yolk. Whisk in the lemon juice and then continue adding the oil while whisking, a little at a time, until all of the oil is blended into the sauce. Adjust the seasoning with lemon juice, salt, and pepper.

2. To make the aioli in a blender: Add the yolk and garlic to the pitcher of the blender. Puree the mixture for a few seconds to combine the ingredients. Add a pinch of salt, and then, with the blender running, pour the oil through the opening in the lid until you have added about half. Add the lemon juice with the machine running, and then resume adding the oil until it has all been blended into the sauce. Adjust the seasoning with lemon juice, salt, and pepper.

3. Aioli can be prepared up to 3 days in advance. Store it in a covered container in the refrigerator.

....

Pesto Genovese
(Italian Basil, Garlic, and Cheese Sauce)

Stir this pungent sauce into soups or risotto, or use it as an ingredient in vinaigrettes, a sandwich spread, or a pizza topping. To use it with pasta, be sure to read the Note following this recipe.

MAKES I CUP, ENOUGH FOR ONE POUND OF DRIED PASTA

2 or 3 garlic cloves, coarsely chopped
2 cups basil (leaves only, no stems or flowers)
⅓ cup pine nuts
½ cup extra-virgin olive oil, plus more to store
⅓ cup grated Parmesan cheese
Kosher salt and freshly ground black pepper, to taste

1. To make the pesto in a food processor: Place the garlic in the food processor and pulse to grind it coarsely. Add the basil, a handful or two at a time, and puree until it is coarsely ground. Add the pine nuts and grind them together with the basil and garlic by pulsing the machine on and off a few times. Scrape down the bowl. With the food processor running, pour the olive oil through the feed tube in a thin stream. Continue to puree the pesto until it is smooth and

light but still has some texture. Transfer the pesto to a bowl and stir in the cheese with a spoon. Season it with salt and pepper.

2. To make the pesto in a mortar and pestle: Pound the garlic in the mortar with the pestle until it is a paste. Add the basil, a handful or two at a time, and pound until the mixture is coarsely ground. Add the pine nuts and pound them into the sauce with the pestle. Add the oil a spoonful at a time while blending it into the basil mixture with the pestle. Continue until all of the oil has been blended into the pesto and it has a smooth but textured consistency. Stir in the cheese, salt, and pepper.

3. The pesto is ready to use now (see Note). To store pesto, place it in a container, top it with a layer of oil, cover it tightly, and keep it in the refrigerator up to 2 days. For longer storage, freeze small containers of pesto for up to 2 months.

NOTE

To serve pesto as a pasta sauce: Cook the pasta according to the package directions. When the pasta is almost completely cooked, ladle out and reserve about ½ cup of the hot pasta water. Drain the pasta well in a colander and transfer it to a heated bowl. Add the pesto and about half of the reserved pasta water. Toss the pasta and pesto together until it is blended. If the pesto is too thick, add the remaining pasta water. Serve at once.

Garlic Scape Pesto

Garlic scapes should be snipped off when they mature so that the energy goes into the garlic bulb and isn't wasted on the stem. They have a short season, usually early summer. They are milder than regular garlic.

MAKES 2 CUPS

1 lb garlic scapes, chopped
¾ cup grated Pecorino Romano cheese
1 cup extra-virgin olive oil, plus more to store
1 tbsp lemon juice
¼ tsp red pepper flakes (optional)
Freshly ground black pepper, to taste

1. To make the pesto in a food processor: Place the scapes and Pecorino Romano in the food processor and pulse to coarsely grind the ingredients. With the food processor running, pour the olive oil through the feed tube in a thin stream. Continue to puree the pesto just until it is smooth and light but still has some texture. Transfer the pesto to a bowl and stir in the lemon juice, red pepper flakes (if using), and black pepper.

2. To make the pesto in a mortar and pestle: Pound the garlic scapes in the mortar with the pestle until they are coarsely ground. Add the Pecorino Romano and pound it into the sauce with the pestle. Add the oil a spoonful at a time while blending it into the sauce with the pestle. Continue until all of the oil has been blended into the pesto and it has a smooth but textured consistency. Stir in the lemon juice, red pepper flakes (if using), and pepper.

3. The pesto is ready to use now. To store pesto, place it in a container, top it with a layer of oil, cover it tightly, and keep it in the refrigerator up to 2 days. For longer storage, freeze small containers of pesto for up to 2 months.

Pilpelchuma
(Pepper Garlic)

Also spelled *pilpelshuma* or *filfel chuma*, this Libyan hot sauce is often compared to harissa. Blend it with a little oil to make a glaze for roasted vegetables, spoon it over scrambled eggs, or add herbs and oil to make a marinade for meats, poultry, or fish. Take care when making this dish; the process is easy, but it is also easy to find yourself inhaling the powdered cayenne while you toast the spices. Covering your mouth and nose with a cloth is a good precaution.

MAKES 1½ CUPS

1 large (⅓ oz) ancho or pasilla chili, or other dried chili
   with a little heat
4 tbsp cayenne
3 tbsp sweet paprika
2 tsp cumin
1½ tsp caraway seeds
20 garlic cloves, peeled
¾ tsp kosher salt
6 tbsp extra-virgin olive oil, plus more to store

1. Place the ancho chili in a small bowl, cover it with hot water, and allow it to soak until tender, about 50 minutes. Drain the chili, discarding the soaking liquid. Cut it into large chunks, discarding the seeds and stem.

2. Add the cayenne, paprika, cumin, and caraway to a dry skillet. Place the skillet over medium heat and toast the spices, swirling the pan or gently stirring the spices, until they are aromatic, about 2 minutes. Immediately transfer the spices to the food processor. Add the chopped chili, the garlic, and salt. Pulse the machine off and on a few times to grind the garlic into a coarse paste. Then,

with the machine running, pour the oil through the feed tube and process the mixture to a thick paste.

3. The pilpelchuma is ready to use now. To store, place the sauce in a jar and cover it with a layer of oil. Close the jar tightly and keep it refrigerated. It will last up to 6 weeks. Replace the layer of oil each time you use some of the pilpelchuma.

....

Ful Medames

This is the national dish of Egypt, where it's frequently eaten for breakfast served with a fried egg and pita bread. Traditionally dried beans were cooked overnight in a copper pot. It's popular throughout the Middle East, where there are many regional variations. Our version includes Aleppo chili flakes, a smoky and moderately hot pepper named for Syria's culinary capital, Aleppo, where it's known as halaby pepper.

MAKES 2 1/2 CUPS

2½ cups cooked or canned peeled fava beans, rinsed and drained
¼ cup fresh lemon juice
¼ cup extra-virgin olive oil, plus more to serve
4 garlic cloves, peeled and mashed
2 tsp ground cumin
½ tsp Aleppo chili powder
Kosher salt and freshly ground black pepper, to taste
2 hard-cooked eggs, cut into 6 wedges each, for garnish
2 tbsp finely chopped parsley, for garnish

1. Place the beans in a saucepan and add enough water to cover them. Bring the water to a simmer over medium heat and cook the beans until they are very hot and tender, about 8 minutes.
2. Use a potato masher or the back of a wooden spoon to mash some of the fava beans and thicken the liquid. Stir in the lemon juice, olive oil, garlic, cumin, chili, salt, and pepper until blended.

3. To serve, pour the beans into a heated serving bowl or individual bowls, garnish the dish with egg wedges and parsley, and drizzle it with olive oil.

....

Zhoug

This garlic-cilantro chutney is popular in Yemen, where it is served as a condiment with a wide array of foods. Make it as fiery as you like by adjusting the type and quantity of chilies you include.

MAKES 3 CUPS

1 tsp cumin seed
1 tsp black peppercorns
4 Thai green chilies minced
4 serrano chilies, seeds and ribs removed, cut into thin strips
2 bunches Italian parsley, roughly chopped (leaves only)
2 bunches cilantro roughly chopped (leaves and tender stems)
12 garlic cloves, finely minced
6 shallots, thinly sliced
2 tsp kosher salt
¼ cup extra-virgin olive oil, or as needed

1. Toast the cumin and peppercorns in dry sauté pan over medium heat until the spices are fragrant but not smoking, about 2 minutes. Immediately transfer them to a spice grinder. When they have cooled, grind them to a powder.
2. Combine the chilies, parsley, cilantro, garlic, and shallots in a food processor. Add the ground spices and salt. Pulse the machine off and on a few times to grind the ingredients coarsely. With the machine running, add the olive oil in a thin stream through the feed tube until the mixture has a coarse but relatively even texture.
3. Zhoug lasts for 2 months (or more). Place it in a jar. Cover it with a layer of oil. Close the jar tightly and store it in the refrigerator. Replace the layer of oil each time you use some.

Lasun Chutney

This pungent condiment from Mumbai, where it is known as *Maharashtra,* is made from garlic, tamarind, and an abundance of dried red chilies. It is frequently served on Bombay *chattis* (street food), especially *vada pay* (fried potato fritters).

MAKES 1 1/2 CUPS

1 cup unsweetened shredded coconut
¼ cup sesame seeds
4 dry-roasted red chilies
1 tbsp roasted salted peanuts
1 head garlic, cloves separated and peeled, coarsely chopped
1 tsp tamarind paste
Kosher salt, to taste

1. Toast the coconut in a dry sauté pan over medium heat, stirring occasionally, until it just begins to turn golden, about 2 minutes. Immediately transfer the coconut to a cool bowl. Return the pan to medium heat, add the sesame seeds, and toast them, stirring occasionally, until they just begin to turn golden, about 2 minutes. Add the sesame seeds to the coconut. Add the chilies to the pan and toast the chilies on both sides until they are softened and flexible, about 1 minute.
2. Combine the chilies and peanuts in a food processor and pulse the mixture until it is coarsely ground. Add the coconut and sesame, garlic, tamarind, and salt. Process the ingredients until they are evenly blended and ground to a coarse texture.
3. This chutney can be prepared up to 2 weeks in advance. Place it in a container, cover it tightly, and store it in the refrigerator.

Georgian Pickled Garlic

This garlic, pickled with pomegranate juice, is a popular snack in the markets of Georgia and Russia. Add it to any pickle or relish plate for a truly different pickle that looks like a bright red jewel on the plate.

MAKES ONE 1-PINT JAR

2 large heads garlic
3 tbsp kosher salt, plus more to sprinkle
½ cup unsweetened pomegranate juice
⅔ cup white wine vinegar
½ tsp black peppercorns
¼ tsp red pepper flakes

1. Remove the outer layers of skin from the garlic head, but leave the cloves unpeeled and the root end still intact. Place the garlic heads in the jar and sprinkle them with the salt.
2. Bring the pomegranate juice and vinegar to a boil in a small saucepan. Remove the pan from the heat and stir in the salt, peppercorns, and pepper flakes. Pour the hot liquid over the garlic. If the garlic is not completely submerged in the pomegranate mixture, make a ball of aluminum foil and put it on top of the garlic. When the jar is closed, the foil will push the garlic under the liquid.
3. Cover the jar tightly and let the garlic ferment in the refrigerator for at least 2 weeks and up to 3 months. The flavor will continue to develop over time.
4. To serve, use a sharp paring knife to cut the garlic cloves away from the root end, about ¼ inch up from the base of the bulb. Pinch the skin at the top of the bulb to pop out the individual cloves.

Ninniku Miso-Zuke

This traditional Japanese recipe ferments garlic in miso (fermented soy paste). The garlic can be served on its own as a pickle or used in any dish that calls for garlic. In this recipe, the aim is to leave the garlic as intact as possible; so here, you are asked to cut away the root end and then peel the garlic by hand rather than use the more typical "smash" technique. Your reward is a unique and delicious garlic pickled in miso and mirin (sweet rice wine).

MAKES ONE 1-PINT JAR

½ lb garlic
1 cup miso
¼ cup mirin

1. Separate the garlic into cloves and then cut off the root ends. Remove the outer skin, then carefully peel off the thin filmy skin that covers each clove.
2. Bring a pot of water to a rolling boil. Add the garlic and let it cook for 2 minutes. Drain the garlic in a colander, pat it dry, and set it aside.
3. Combine the miso paste and the mirin in a bowl with a fork. Spread a small amount of the miso mixture in the bottom of a glass jar. Add a single layer of garlic cloves on top of the miso, then cover the cloves with another layer of the miso mixture. Continue this layering process until all of the garlic and miso mixture has been used. Make sure that all of the garlic cloves are covered with miso.
4. Cover the jar tightly and let the garlic ferment in the refrigerator at least 10 days and up to 3 months. Check the jar daily during the first 4 or 5 days of fermentation. If the lid is bulging, open the jar to release the pressure.
5. To serve, use a small spoon or fork to pull out as many cloves as you

need. Scrape away or rinse off the miso mixture, blot the cloves dry with paper towels, and serve. You can also wash the cloves before drying and serving them.

....

Kimchi
(Korean Fermented Cabbage)

Patience is a virtue when it comes to fermenting kimchi. The Koreans traditionally bury a crock of cabbage to ferment underground for several months before breaking the seal. You can eat this kimchi anytime after the initial fermentation of 2 to 3 days, but the longer you wait, the better the flavor.

MAKES FOUR I-QUART JARS OR ONE I-GALLON JAR

2 heads Napa cabbage
1 cup plus 1 tbsp coarse sea salt or kosher salt
8 cups water
1 head garlic, cloves separated and peeled
1 piece (2 inches) ginger root, sliced
¼ cup fish sauce or Korean salted shrimp
1 daikon (Asian radish), peeled and grated
1 bunch green onions, cut into 1-inch lengths
⅓ cup Korean chili powder (or substitute equal parts
   cayenne and paprika)
1 tsp sugar (optional)
Sesame oil, to serve
Sesame seeds (optional), to serve

1. Cut the cabbages in half lengthwise and then into 2-inch wedges. Put the cabbage in a large bowl. Stir together 1 cup of the salt and water until the salt dissolves, and pour it over the cabbage. Let the cabbage soak for at least 4 and up to 8 hours.

2. Combine the garlic, ginger, and fish sauce or shrimp in a food processor or blender, and puree the mixture until the ingredients are finely minced.

3. To make the daikon filling: Combine the radish, green onions, garlic mixture, chili powder, 1 tablespoon salt, and sugar (if using) in a large bowl. Toss gently but thoroughly using tongs or with gloved hands.

4. Remove the cabbage from the salt water, rinse it thoroughly with cold water, and drain the leaves in a colander. Squeeze the cabbage to remove as much water as possible. Working with one wedge of cabbage at a time, remove the largest outer leaf to use as a wrapper. Stuff a little of the daikon mixture between the leaves, working from the largest leaves on the outside to the smaller leaves on the inside. Wrap the reserved leaf around the rest of the cabbage. Place the rolls in a 1-gallon canning jar (or among four 1-quart jars), pressing the cabbage down firmly to remove any air pockets.

5. Cover the jar tightly and let the kimchi ferment in a cool place (about 65°F) for 2 or 3 days. Check the jar(s) daily. If the lid is bulging, open the jar to release the pressure. Continue to ferment the kimchi in the refrigerator for at least 2 weeks and up to 3 months. The flavor will continue to develop over time.

6. Serve the kimchi, drizzled with sesame oil and sprinkled with sesame seeds, if desired.

BREAD, PIZZA, AND PASTA

Cheesy Garlic Bread

The butter-cheese-herb spread in this recipe is delightful on sandwiches or as a filling for an omelet; so as long as you are mixing it up, you might want to double the ingredients to have more on hand. You can even shape it into balls and roll it in nuts for a classic cheese ball for your next get-together.

MAKES 8 SERVINGS

½ cup butter, room temperature
4 garlic cloves, crushed
¼ lb grated mozzarella
¼ lb grated sharp cheddar
3 tbsp chopped parsley
2 tbsp chopped basil
Pinch cracked black pepper or red pepper flakes
1 large loaf ciabatta bread

1. Preheat the oven to 400°F.
2. Combine the butter, garlic, mozzarella, cheddar, parsley, basil, and

pepper in a food processor or in a bowl with a wooden spoon until the ingredients are evenly blended.

3. Cut the ciabatta loaf into ½-inch-thick slices, slicing at an angle and cutting only two-thirds of the way through the loaf, leaving the bottom third intact. Spread the filling mixture evenly between the slices. Wrap the loaf loosely with foil, folding up the corners and edges to cover it completely.

4. Place the wrapped loaf on a baking sheet and bake it until the filling is melted, about 20 minutes. Unwrap the loaf and return it to the oven to bake for another 5 minutes.

5. Serve immediately.

....

Pampushky

These Russian garlic buns are traditionally served with borscht, but they are perfect with any hearty soup or stew or as a replacement for a standard garlic bread with your favorite pasta dinner.

MAKES 12 ROLLS

¾ oz (1½ packets) active dry yeast
2 cups tepid water
3½ cups flour
1 tbsp sugar
1 tsp kosher salt
1 large egg yolk
2 tbsp milk
1 tbsp vegetable oil

Garlic Sauce
1 tbsp olive oil
1 tbsp water
3 garlic cloves, minced
Pinch of salt

1. Combine the yeast and water in the bowl of a stand mixer or a large mixing bowl. Let the yeast rest until it is foamy, about 5 minutes.

2. Add the flour, sugar, and salt to the yeast mixture and stir it with a dough hook on low speed or a wooden spoon until the dough is evenly moistened, 3 to 4 minutes; it will be heavy and shaggy looking. Knead the dough with the dough hook on medium speed until it is very smooth, about 4 minutes, or knead it by hand on a floured work surface, about 10 minutes.

3. Shape the dough into a round and put it in a lightly oiled bowl. Cover the bowl with a clean cloth or plastic wrap and let the dough rise in a warm place until nearly doubled, about 1 hour. Fold the dough over on itself two or three times and turn it out onto a floured work surface. Cut the dough into 12 equal pieces and shape each piece into a smooth round. Place the rolls into a lightly greased rectangular baking pan (9 x 13). Cover the rolls with a clean cloth or plastic wrap and let them rise until they nearly double in size, about 30 minutes.

4. Preheat the oven to 350°F while the rolls are rising. Whisk together the egg yolk, milk, and oil. Brush this mixture liberally over the tops and sides of the rolls.

5. To make the Garlic Sauce, whisk together the oil, water, garlic, and salt.

6. Bake the rolls until the tops and bottoms are golden brown and they are baked through, about 20 minutes. Brush the Garlic Sauce evenly over the rolls and return them to the oven for an addition 2 minutes.

7. Serve the rolls hot from the oven.

Pizza Escarole

This meatless Neapolitan dish is most commonly served on Christmas Eve, when religious tradition prohibits the eating of meat. Capers preserved in salt have a more delicate, flowery flavor than those preserved in brine, but they can be substituted if necessary. The best salted capers are said to come from the Sicilian island of Pantelleria.

MAKES 6 SERVINGS

2 lb (2 heads) escarole, separated into leaves
2 tbsp olive oil
3 garlic cloves, peeled and thinly sliced
10 black olives, pitted and sliced
1 (2 oz) can flat anchovies, chopped
½ cup pine nuts
½ cup dark raisins
1 tbsp salted capers, rinsed and drained
Freshly ground black pepper, to taste
1 lb pizza dough

1. Preheat the oven to 400°F.
2. Bring a large pot of salted water to a boil. Add the escarole, stir to submerge it completely, and simmer until tender, about 5 minutes. Drain the escarole in a colander and rinse it with cool water. When the escarole is cool enough to handle, squeeze it well to remove excess water and then chop it coarsely.
3. Heat the olive oil in a sauté pan over medium-high heat. Add the garlic, olives, anchovies, and pine nuts, and sauté, stirring frequently, until the garlic begins to turn golden, about 1 minute. Add the escarole and cook it uncovered, stirring frequently, until it is very hot and flavorful and most of the liquid is cooked away, about 10 minutes. Stir in the raisins and capers. Season the mixture with pepper. Let the filling cool to room temperature while preparing the dough.

4. Divide the dough into two pieces: One piece should be about two-thirds of the dough and the other about one-third. Roll the larger piece out into a 16-inch round and transfer it to a 12-inch round baking dish or pan to line the bottom and sides. Fill the dough with the escarole mixture. Roll out the remaining dough into a 12-inch round for the top crust. Pinch the edges of the dough together to seal the top and bottom together.

5. Bake the pizza until the crust is golden brown, about 25 minutes. Let it rest for 5 minutes before cutting it into wedges. Serve immediately.

....

Spaghetti Aglio e Olio

There is an art to combining pasta with a sauce, and timing is everything. Start the garlic as soon as you have the pasta in the water, and everything will be ready at the same time. Don't skip the pasta water; it makes all the difference between a creamy sauce that coats each strand and an oily, slippery one.

**MAKES 6 FIRST-COURSE SERVINGS OR
4 MAIN-COURSE SERVINGS**

1 lb uncooked spaghetti
2 tsp kosher salt, divided
8 garlic cloves, cut into thin slivers
⅓ cup extra-virgin olive oil
1 tbsp crushed red pepper flakes
1 cup grated Parmesan cheese, plus more to serve
½ cup minced fresh parsley

1. Bring a large pot of water to a boil over high heat. Add the spaghetti and 1 teaspoon salt; stir the pasta a few times to submerge and separate the strands. Cook the spaghetti until it is just tender to the bite (al dente), about 8 minutes (or according to package directions).

2. Reserve about 1 cup of the pasta cooking water. Drain the pasta well in a colander.

3. While the pasta is boiling, prepare the garlic. Add the oil to a deep sauté pan. Add the garlic and place the pan over medium-low heat. Let the garlic cook, stirring occasionally, until the garlic is crisp and light golden brown, 5 to 6 minutes. Add the red pepper flakes and cook for 30 seconds.

4. Add the reserved pasta cooking water to the oil and bring the mixture to a boil over medium-high heat. Lower the heat to medium, add the remaining 1 teaspoon of salt, and simmer until the liquid is reduced by about one-third, about 5 minutes.

5. Add the drained spaghetti to the garlic sauce and toss them together over medium heat until the pasta is evenly coated. Remove the pan from the heat and stir in the Parmesan and parsley. Serve the spaghetti at once in a heated pasta bowl or individual pasta plates. Serve with additional Parmesan on the side, if desired.

SOUPS

~~~

Ajo Blanco

Soups that use up stale bread are a staple around the world. In this case, the bread is featured in a white, cold garlic soup with grapes and almonds from the Andalusia region of Spain. Be sure to choose a bread with some definite texture like a *miche* or other peasant or farmhouse-style bread. This dish is sometimes called "white gazpacho."

MAKES 6 SERVINGS

3 cups cubed peasant-style white bread, crust removed and dried
    uncovered overnight at room temperature
3 cups cold water, divided, or as needed
2¼ cups blanched whole almonds
3 garlic cloves, or to taste, crushed to a paste
½ cup extra-virgin olive oil, plus extra for garnish
Kosher salt, to taste
3 tbsp sherry vinegar
18 seedless green grapes, halved, for garnish

1. Put the bread cubes in a bowl and pour 1 cup of the water over them, tossing the bread to dampen it evenly. Let the bread soak for about 15 minutes.

2. Grind the almonds very fine in a food processor, pulsing the machine off and on and scraping down the bowl to grind them evenly. Add the soaked bread, garlic, and olive oil, and puree to a thick, coarse paste. With the machine running, gradually add as much of the remaining 2 cups of water as needed through the lid or feed tube until the soup has a light, creamy consistency. Season with salt to taste.

3. Transfer the mixture to a container, stir in the vinegar, and chill the soup in the refrigerator for at least 3 and up to 12 hours before serving.

4. Serve the soup in chilled bowls or cups, garnished with green grapes and drizzled with olive oil.

....

Pink Garlic Soup

This delicate soup is served at the Rose Garlic Festival in Lautrec, France, accompanied by glasses of rosé wine. You need Lautrec pink garlic for an authentic version, but other varieties of garlic work too.

MAKES 8 SERVINGS

1 large egg yolk
1 tsp water
1 tsp Dijon-style mustard
¾ cup extra-virgin olive oil
Kosher salt and freshly ground black pepper, to taste
8 cups water
10 Lautrec pink garlic cloves, peeled and crushed
1 large egg white, lightly beaten
6 oz uncooked vermicelli pasta

1. Start by making a mayonnaise: Whisk the egg yolk, water, and mustard together in a bowl. While whisking, gradually add the olive oil in a thin stream until all of the oil is incorporated; it will be thicker than a typical mayonnaise at this point. Season the mayonnaise with salt and pepper to taste.

2. To make the soup base: In a soup pot, bring the water to a boil over high heat. Add the garlic and egg white. Reduce the heat to medium and let the soup simmer for 3 minutes. Add the vermicelli and cook it until it is tender, another 3 minutes.

3. Ladle about 1 cup of the hot soup into the mayonnaise and stir, then combine the mayonnaise with the remaining hot soup.

4. Serve the soup at once in heated soup bowls.

....

Elizabeth David's Garlic Soup

Elizabeth David opened up the world of garlic in England when she published *A Book of Mediterranean Food* in the 1950s. This dish proves her point that, when it comes to garlic, more is less. A whole head of garlic lessens rather than increases garlic's pungency—and simmered for an hour, the garlic becomes mild and sweet.

MAKES 4 SERVINGS

1 head garlic, separated into cloves, unpeeled
5 cups chicken broth
1 tbsp butter
1 tbsp extra-virgin olive oil
1 medium onion, chopped
Pinch of saffron threads, crumbled
Kosher salt and freshly ground black pepper, to taste
4 large slices French bread (see Note)
1 garlic clove (see Note)
4 poached eggs (see Note)
2 tsp white wine vinegar (see Note)

1. Combine the garlic and chicken broth in a soup pot, bring them to a simmer over low heat, then cover and simmer until the broth is very flavorful and the garlic is very tender, about 1 hour.

2. Strain the broth into a second pot. When the garlic is cool enough to handle, slip the garlic skins from the cloves and put the cloves into the bowl of a food processor.

3. Heat the butter and oil in a sauté pan over medium-high heat until it stops foaming. Add the onion and saffron, then sauté, stirring frequently, until the onion is soft, about 4 minutes. Add the onion to the garlic in the food processor.

4. Puree the garlic and onion with about 2 cups of the broth until it is very smooth. Return the puree to the rest of the broth and return the soup to a simmer before serving. Season with salt and pepper to taste.

5. Serve the soup in heated soup bowls topped with a slice of toasted bread and a poached egg (see Note).

NOTE

To prepare the toasted bread for this soup, cut 4 slices from a baguette at a slight angle, about ¼ inch thick. Cut a garlic clove in half and rub the cut sides over the bread. Toast under a broiler until golden brown, turn once, and toast on the second side.

To poach the eggs, bring a large pot of water to a boil over high heat. The water should be a least 4 inches deep in the pot. Reduce the heat to medium and add 2 teaspoons white wine vinegar. Crack the eggs into a cup of small plate and then slide the egg into the water. Let the eggs poach to the desired doneness, about 3 minutes for set whites with a soft, runny yolk. Lift the eggs from the water with a slotted spoon and blot briefly on paper towels.

Sopa de Ajo Castellana
(Castilian Garlic Soup)

King Alphonso XI of Castile (1311–50) hated garlic so much that he made it a statute of knighthood that if a knight were to eat it, he would not be allowed to appear before the king for at least a month. The late king would be horrified to learn that one of Spain's most beloved garlic dishes, Sopa de Ajo Castellana, is named for his province. This recipe is adapted from *The New Mediterranean Diet Cookbook* by Nancy Harmon Jenkins.

The poached eggs are optional, but if you include them, breaking the yolk into the soup adds an incredible richness as well as a beautiful golden color.

MAKES 4 SERVINGS

¼ cup extra-virgin olive oil

4 heads garlic, cloves separated and peeled (enough to make about 1 cup or ½ lb peeled garlic cloves)

1 tsp red pepper flakes

4½ cups chicken broth

½ cup Spanish amontillado or oloroso sherry

1 pinch ground cumin

1 pinch saffron threads

Kosher salt and freshly ground pepper, to taste

4 slices baguette (see Note, page 150)

1 garlic clove

4 poached eggs (see Note, page 150)

Freshly shaved or grated Manchego cheese (optional)

1. Heat the oil in a heavy soup pot over low heat. Add the garlic and sauté, stirring frequently, until the garlic is tender but not browned, about 10 minutes. Lift the garlic out of the oil with a slotted spoon, transfer it to a bowl, and set it aside.

2. Stir the red pepper flakes into the hot oil in the soup pot over medium heat until it is aromatic, about 15 seconds, then add the broth and sherry. Stir in the cumin and saffron and bring the soup to a simmer. Return the garlic to the soup and use a potato masher or the back of a wooden spoon to mash the garlic into a paste. Simmer the soup until it is very flavorful, about 15 minutes. Season it with salt and pepper.

3. Serve the soup very hot in heated soup bowls. If desired, float a piece of garlic toast on top of each serving and top the bread with an egg (see Note on page 150). Add grated Manchego, if using.

....

Garlic Cheddar Ale Soup

Doubling up the garlic by using both sautéed and roasted garlic gives this rich soup a nearly addictive appeal. Look for a heady ale with plenty of flavor for a perfect match with the garlic. Have some on hand to enjoy with the soup, as well as hearty rolls or bread for dunking.

MAKES 4 TO 6 SERVINGS

½ cup unsalted butter
1 yellow onion, diced
5 garlic cloves, minced
⅔ cups all-purpose flour
2 cups vegetable or chicken broth
1 cup ale (IPA is recommended)
1 cup whole milk
3 heads garlic, roasted and pureed
1 tbsp smoked paprika
½ tsp ground cumin
1 lb aged sharp cheddar cheese, grated
Kosher salt and freshly ground black pepper, to taste
Chopped fresh chives, for garnish (optional)

1. Melt the butter in a heavy soup pot over low heat. Add the onion and the minced garlic, and sauté, stirring frequently, until the onion is tender but not browned, about 8 minutes. Stir in flour and cook, stirring constantly, to make a smooth, thick paste, about 2 minutes.

2. Pour in the broth gradually in a slow stream, whisking constantly. Add the ale and the milk in the same manner, whisking until the soup is blended and smooth. Stir in the pureed garlic, paprika, and cumin. Bring the soup to a simmer over medium heat, stirring frequently, until it is thickened and flavorful, about 20 minutes. Remove the pot from the heat and stir in the grated cheese. Season with salt and pepper.

3. Serve the soup at once in heated soup bowls garnished with chives (if using).

....

Knoblauchcremesuppe

This Austrian creamy garlic soup has many different interpretations. Some include potatoes for body; others call for vinegar or nutmeg as a seasoning. This version includes all the traditional elements—garlic, onion, flour, and milk—garnished with croutons and parsley.

MAKES 6 SERVINGS

¾ cup cubed bread for croutons
3 tbsp unsalted butter
10 garlic cloves, finely minced
¼ cup all-purpose flour
¾ cup milk
1½ cups chicken (or vegetable) stock
2 tbsp chopped parsley, plus additional for garnish

1. To make the croutons, preheat the oven to 350°F. Spread the bread cubes on a baking sheet. Toast the bread cubes in the oven, turning them occasionally to brown evenly, until they are crisp and golden brown, about 10 minutes.

2. Melt the butter in a heavy soup pot over low heat. Add the garlic and sauté, stirring frequently, until the garlic is tender but not browned, about 8 minutes. Stir the flour into the garlic and cook, stirring constantly, to make a smooth, thick paste, about 2 minutes.

3. Pour in the milk gradually in a slow stream, whisking constantly. Add the chicken stock in the same manner, whisking until the soup is blended and smooth. Bring the soup to a simmer over medium heat, stirring frequently, until it is thickened and flavorful, about 20 minutes.

4. Just before serving, stir the parsley into the soup. Serve the soup at once in heated soup bowls garnished with croutons.

....

Mirao
(Cristoforo Colombo's Chicken Soup)

Chef Cesare Casella, the dean of Italian studies at the International Culinary Center, says that this soup was a favorite of Christopher Columbus. This version is adapted from Casella's recipe.

MAKES 8 SERVINGS

5 tbsp extra-virgin olive oil, plus more to finish
1 cup thinly sliced onions
½ cup diagonally sliced carrots
¼ cup sliced garlic cloves
1 average-sized (3 to 4 lb) chicken, cut into 6 to 8 pieces
Kosher salt and freshly ground black pepper, to taste
½ cup brandy
6 cups water, or as needed
cheesecloth (6-inch square)

6 whole cloves

3 bay leaves

½ cinnamon stick

1 whole nutmeg

2 sprigs rosemary

1 stalk celery, cut into 3-inch pieces

¼ cup chopped flat leaf parsley

16 slices day-old baguette

1 garlic clove, peeled and halved

½ cup grated Parmesan cheese

1. Heat the oil in a soup pot over medium-high heat. Add the onion, carrots, and garlic and sauté, stirring frequently, until the onion is golden, about 8 minutes.

2. Season the chicken pieces with salt and pepper and add them to the pot. Cook, turning the chicken occasionally, until the chicken and vegetables are lightly browned. Add the brandy and reduce it by half. Add enough of the 6 cups of water to cover the chicken by about 1 inch, and season it with salt and pepper.

3. Make a spice sachet: Cut a 6-inch square piece of cheesecloth and use it to wrap up the cloves, bay leaves, cinnamon stick, nutmeg, and rosemary.

4. Add the sachet and celery to the soup. When the soup returns to a simmer, reduce the heat to low and simmer until the chicken is fully cooked and tender, 45 minutes to 1 hour.

5. Remove and discard the sachet and celery. Lift the chicken pieces from the soup with a slotted spoon. When the chicken is cool enough to handle, remove the skin and bones and discard them. Shred the meat into pieces.

6. Skim the soup well to remove any fat on the surface (see Note). Return the chicken to the soup and bring it to a simmer. Season it with salt and pepper and stir in the parsley.

7. Preheat the broiler and rub the bread slices with the halved garlic. Toast the bread until it is golden brown on both sides. Place 1

toasted slice in each of 8 ovenproof soup bowls. Top the toast with a ladle of the soup then another slice of toast. Drizzle the toast with a little olive oil and sprinkle it evenly with Parmesan. Put the bowls on a baking sheet and broil until the tops are golden brown and bubbly, about 2 minutes. Serve at once.

NOTE

If you have time, let the soup chill for several hours in the refrigerator. The fat will harden and lift easily from the surface. Bring the soup back to a simmer before continuing with step 6.

....

Garlic, Escarole, and White Bean Soup

This soup delivers the essence of garlic because the cloves are smashed but left whole. You can either pluck them out of the soup before you serve it or leave the cloves to enjoy as part of the soup. They will be sweet, nutty, and very tender by the time the soup finishes simmering.

MAKES 4 TO 6 SERVINGS

1 tbsp olive oil
8 large garlic cloves, peeled, flattened
1 cup chopped onion
1 carrot, finely diced
1 teaspoon dried oregano
1 teaspoon dried basil
3 cups (packed) coarsely chopped escarole (about ½ large head)
4 cups (or more) vegetable or chicken broth
2 cups cooked or canned white beans, rinsed and drained
1 (14½ oz) can diced tomatoes, drained
½ cup uncooked spaghetti broken into 2-inch pieces
¼ cup Pesto Genovese (page 130)

1. Heat the oil in a soup pot over medium-high heat. Add the garlic and cook, stirring constantly, until the cloves are lightly browned and aromatic, about 2 minutes. Add the onion, carrot, oregano, and basil, and sauté, stirring frequently, until the onions are golden, about 5 minutes.

2. Add the escarole and stir until the escarole wilts and is evenly coated with oil. Add the broth, beans, and tomatoes. Bring the soup to a simmer and then reduce the heat to medium. Add the spaghetti and continue to simmer until the spaghetti is fully cooked and the soup is flavorful, about 30 minutes.

3. Just before serving, stir in the pesto (see page 130). Serve in a heated soup tureen or individual bowls.

....

Caldeirada

This Portuguese fish stew is also popular in Brazil, where cilantro is added. The recipe calls for half flaky white fish and half flavorful oily fish.

MAKES 4 SERVINGS

¾ lb flaky white fish (such as cod, halibut, and/or tilapia)
¾ lb oily fish (such as mackerel, bluefish, and/or trout)
1½ tsp kosher salt, divided
1½ lb boiling potatoes, peeled and quartered
1 qt water
1 onion, quartered
2 bay leaves

Ajada Sauce
¼ cup extra-virgin olive oil
4 garlic cloves, peeled and chopped
2 tbsp sweet pimentón (Spanish paprika)
2 tbsp wine vinegar

1. Cut the fish fillets into chunks and place them in a bowl. Sprinkle the cut fish with ½ teaspoon salt and toss to evenly coat the pieces. Set them aside.

2. Put the potatoes in a deep, heavy-bottomed soup pot. Add the water, onion, bay leaves, and the remaining 1 teaspoon salt. Bring the water to a boil over high heat, then reduce the heat, cover the pot, and simmer the potatoes for 10 minutes.

3. Add the fish, replace the cover, and continue to simmer until the potatoes are tender and the fish just flakes, about 15 minutes. Remove and discard the bay leaf.

4. To make the Ajada Sauce: Heat the oil in a small skillet over medium-high heat. Add the garlic and sauté, stirring constantly, until golden, about 1 minute. Remove the pan from the heat and stir in the pimentón and vinegar.

5. Lift the potatoes and fish from the soup, and transfer them to a heated soup tureen or soup bowl. Stir the Ajada Sauce into the broth and return it to a boil before pouring it over the fish and potatoes. Serve at once.

SALADS AND SALAD DRESSINGS

Pantzaria Salata

The combination of beets and garlic is a Greek classic. Top this delicious concoction with garlic-yogurt sauce.

MAKES 6 SERVINGS

2 lb fresh red beets (or 2 cans of sliced beets, drained)
3 garlic cloves, minced
½ cup extra-virgin olive oil
¼ cup red wine vinegar
Kosher salt and freshly ground black pepper, to taste

Garlic-Yogurt Sauce
8 oz plain Greek yogurt
1 garlic clove, minced
1 tbsp freshly squeezed lemon juice
Kosher salt and freshly ground pepper, to taste

1. To prepare the beets: Trim the leaves from the beets, leaving about 1 inch of the stems attached. Scrub the beets lightly and place them

in a pot with enough cold water to cover them by about 2 inches. Place the pot over medium-high heat, add the salt, and bring the water to a boil. Boil the beets until they are tender enough to pierce easily with the tip of a paring knife, about 40 minutes. Drain the beets in a colander, and when they are cool enough to handle, trim away the stem and root ends and slip off the skin (it should come away easily, but use a paring knife to cut the skin away if necessary). Cut the beets into slices, about ¼ inch thick.

2. Transfer the sliced beets to a bowl and add the garlic, olive oil, vinegar, salt, and pepper. Toss to coat the beets evenly. Marinate the beets in the refrigerator for at least 8 hours before serving.

3. To make the Garlic-Yogurt Sauce: Whisk the yogurt, garlic, and lemon juice together in a bowl. Season the mixture with salt and pepper. (If made in advance, store the sauce in a covered container in the refrigerator for up to 2 days.)

4. Serve the salad chilled or at room temperature and top it with a dollop of the Garlic-Yogurt Sauce.

NOTE

These beets will last at least 1 week in the refrigerator, and the flavor continues to deepen and develop as it rests.

Zaalouk

The technique of roasting vegetables at a low temperature produces rich flavors and silky textures that shine in this delicious Moroccan eggplant salad. The addition of raw garlic to the dish is a perfect counterpoint, adding snap and bite to the dish and complementing the flavors of the roasted vegetables.

MAKES 2 CUPS OR 6 APPETIZER SERVINGS

Olive oil to prepare the baking sheet
1 large eggplant (or 2 medium)
2 medium green bell peppers
1 jalapeño, poblano, or other chili (optional)
3 large tomatoes, peeled, seeded, and chopped
⅓ cup extra-virgin olive oil
4 garlic cloves, minced
2 tsp mild paprika
1 tsp ground cumin
1 tsp kosher salt
¼ tsp freshly ground black pepper
⅓ cup water
2 tbsp lemon juice, or to taste
⅓ cup chopped fresh cilantro and/or parsley
Kosher salt and freshly ground black pepper, to taste

1. Preheat the oven to 350°F. Brush a baking sheet liberally with olive oil.
2. Slice the eggplant in half lengthwise. Place it on the baking sheet, cut side facing down. Slice the green peppers and the chili (if using) in half lengthwise and pull out the seeds. Place the peppers and the chili on the baking sheet cut side facing down. Press the peppers and chili flat with the palm of your hand so they roast evenly.

3. Add the tomatoes and roast the vegetables until the eggplant is soft and yields to the touch and the skin on the peppers has browned and blistered, 35 to 40 minutes.

4. When the vegetables are cool enough to handle, pull the skins from the peppers and chili (if using) and cut them into strips; set aside. Scoop the flesh from the eggplant, discarding the skin and any large pockets of seeds. Chop the eggplant coarsely and set it aside.

5. Heat the olive oil in a deep skillet over medium heat. Add the garlic and sauté, stirring constantly, until aromatic, 30 seconds. Add the paprika, cumin, salt, and pepper and stir until combined. Add the peppers, eggplant, tomatoes, and water. Stir well, mashing the eggplant with the back of your spoon or with a potato masher to break it up. Bring the mixture to a simmer, and then cover the skillet and reduce the heat to low. Simmer, stirring occasionally, until it is thickened and flavorful, about 20 minutes.

6. Add the lemon juice and continue cooking, uncovered, to reduce the mixture to a heavy consistency, another 5 minutes. The Zaalouk can be prepared up to this point and then stored in a covered container in the refrigerator for up to 5 days.

7. Just before serving, stir in the parsley or cilantro and season the dish with additional lemon juice, salt, or pepper. Transfer the Zaalouk to a serving dish and drizzle it with olive oil.

8. Serve cold or at room temperature, accompanied with toasted pita wedges.

....

Garlic-Scented Tomato Salad

Marcella Hazan taught millions of Americans how to prepare the simple fresh food of Italy at a time when our idea of Italian food was a can of Chef Boy-Ar-Dee Beef Ravioli. In her 2004 cookbook, *Marcella Says . . .* , she wrote, "The unbalanced use of garlic is the single greatest cause of failure in would-be Italian cooking. It must remain a shadowy background presence. It cannot take over the show." This delectable recipe for tomato salad perfumed with garlic embodies Hazan's philosophy perfectly.

MAKES 4 SERVINGS

4 or 5 garlic cloves, peeled and mashed

2 tbsp choice-quality red wine vinegar, or more to taste

1 tsp kosher salt, or more to taste

2 lb fresh, ripe plum or slicing tomatoes, peeled (see Note)

12 large fresh basil leaves

3 tbsp extra-virgin olive oil

1. Combine the garlic, vinegar, and salt in a small bowl until the vinegar has a good garlic flavor, 25 to 30 minutes.
2. Arrange the tomato slices in a serving dish or platter. Strain the garlic-infused vinegar over the tomatoes. Tear the basil leaves into pieces and scatter over the tomatoes. Drizzle the salad with olive oil, and serve at room temperature.

NOTE

To peel tomatoes, you can either cut the skin away with a sharp paring knife or blanch them briefly to loosen the skin as follows: Bring a pot of water to a rolling boil. Score an "X" into the bottom of each tomato, without cutting too deeply into the flesh. Lower the tomatoes into the boiling water, a few at a time, and cook them for 15 to 20 seconds. Immediately lift the tomatoes out of the water and transfer them to a bowl filled with ice water. Continue until all of the tomatoes are blanched. Drain the tomatoes and then pull the skin away.

··

Frisée with Burnt Garlic Vinaigrette

This Spanish salad is topped with garlic "chips" that have been cooked at a low heat until they are a rich deep brown that's almost, but not quite, burnt.

MAKES 6 TO 8 SERVINGS

7 to 8 cups frisée, torn into bite-size pieces
4 tbsp olive oil
7 or 8 garlic cloves, thickly sliced
½ lb smoked Spanish-style chorizo sausage, sliced
3 tbsp sherry vinegar
Kosher salt and freshly ground black pepper, to taste
¼ cup grated Manchego cheese (optional)

1. Put the frisée in a large salad bowl.
2. To make the garlic chips, add the oil to a small skillet. Add the garlic and place the skillet over medium heat. Let the garlic cook, stirring occasionally, until the garlic is crisp and light golden brown, 2 to 3 minutes. Take the skillet off of the heat. Lift the garlic from the oil with a slotted spoon and transfer it to paper toweling to drain.
3. Return skillet to the heat. Add the chorizo and cook it until it is warmed through but not browned, about 1 minute per side. Add it to the frisée.
4. Stir the vinegar into the skillet and season the dressing with salt and pepper to taste. Pour the dressing over the frisée and chorizo and toss them until they are coated evenly.
5. Just before serving, scatter the garlic chips and Manchego (if using) over the salad. Serve at once.

Roasted Garlic and Quinoa Salad

This salad draws its inspiration from tabbouleh, the Middle Eastern salad of couscous, parsley, and garlic. Quinoa is a protein-packed replacement for couscous, but you can make this salad with other grains, if you prefer. Barley and farro are two great options. Or, try a pasta instead, such as fregola or tubettini.

MAKES 6 TO 8 SERVINGS

1 head garlic, roasted and pureed
¼ cup red wine vinegar
3 tbsp fresh lemon juice
2 tsp Dijon mustard
4 tbsp extra-virgin olive oil, divided
Kosher salt and freshly ground black pepper, to taste
1 pt cherry tomatoes, halved
1 cup water
¾ cup quinoa
2 cups baby spinach or arugula
Black olives (optional)
Feta cheese (optional)

1. Preheat the oven to 400°F.
2. Combine the garlic, vinegar, lemon juice, mustard, and 3 tablespoons of the olive oil in a bowl and whisk the ingredients to combine them. Season with salt and pepper. Set the bowl aside.
3. Put the tomatoes on a baking sheet, drizzle them with 1 tablespoon of the olive oil, and sprinkle them with a pinch of salt and pepper. Roast the tomatoes until they darken and have a rich aroma, about 15 minutes. Cool them to room temperature.
4. Bring the water to a boil in a small saucepan over high heat. Add the quinoa. Stir once or twice and return the water to a boil. Turn off the heat and cover the pot tightly. Let the quinoa steam until it is

tender, about 20 minutes. Fluff the quinoa with a fork and transfer it to a salad bowl. Let the quinoa cool to room temperature.

5. Add the tomatoes, spinach or arugula, black olives, and feta (if using). Stir the dressing to recombine and then pour it over the salad. Toss all of the ingredients until they are evenly coated. Serve the salad directly from the salad bowl or on individual plates.

....

Creamy Garlic Dressing

Store-bought salad dressing can't compete with homemade. Creamy garlic dressings have been a steakhouse standard for years, and this one is just as delicious on a wedge of iceberg as it is on a grilled steak salad.

MAKES 1 1/2 CUPS

1 large egg yolk
⅓ cup white balsamic vinegar
3 garlic cloves, minced
½ tsp Dijon mustard
½ tsp kosher salt
¼ tsp freshly ground black pepper
1 cup extra-virgin olive oil

1. Whisk the egg yolk, vinegar, garlic, mustard, salt, and pepper together in a bowl or blend them in a mini-food processor. While whisking or with the machine running, gradually add the olive oil and blend the ingredients until the vinaigrette is combined and thickened. Taste and adjust it with additional salt and pepper.

2. The dressing can be prepared up to 2 days in advance. Store it in a covered container in the refrigerator. Shake or whisk the dressing well to recombine it before serving.

Roasted Garlic Vinaigrette

The mellow roasted garlic makes this dressing smooth and slightly sweet. It complements everything from frisée and grilled asparagus to smoked Spanish chorizo sausage and roasted pork.

MAKES I CUP

¼ cup red wine vinegar
1 head garlic, roasted and pureed
1 tbsp fresh lime juice
1 tsp Dijon mustard
1 tbsp honey
½ tsp kosher salt
¼ tsp freshly ground black pepper
½ cup olive oil

1. Whisk the vinegar, garlic, lime juice, mustard, honey, salt, and pepper together in a bowl or blend them in a mini-food processor. While whisking or with the machine running, gradually add the olive oil and blend the ingredients until the vinaigrette is combined and thickened. Taste and adjust with additional salt and pepper.
2. The vinaigrette can be prepared up to 2 days in advance. Store it in a covered container in the refrigerator. Shake or whisk the vinaigrette well to recombine it before serving.

Lemon Garlic Vinaigrette

This easy vinaigrette (made from readily available ingredients) gets a subtle punch from Dijon mustard. It can be served over grilled vegetables, boiled potatoes, freshly picked tomatoes, or a variety of greens.

MAKES I CUP

¼ cup fresh lemon juice
4 garlic cloves, minced
2 tsp Dijon mustard
1 tsp finely grated lemon zest
½ tsp kosher salt, or to taste
¼ tsp freshly ground black pepper, or to taste
¾ cup extra-virgin olive oil

1. Whisk the lemon juice, garlic, mustard, lemon zest, salt, and pepper together in a bowl or blend them in a mini-food processor. While whisking or with the machine running, gradually add the olive oil and blend the ingredients until the vinaigrette is combined and thickened. Taste and adjust with additional salt and pepper.
2. The vinaigrette can be prepared up to 2 days in advance. Store it in a covered container in the refrigerator. Shake or whisk the vinaigrette well to recombine it before serving.

Asian Vinaigrette

Asian flavors make this dressing a natural for salad greens, cabbage, noodles, or seared tuna. The optional dash of hot chili oil gives it a nice kick.

MAKES 1 CUP

4 garlic cloves, minced
1 tsp freshly grated ginger
3 tbsp rice wine vinegar
3 tbsp soy sauce
1 tbsp honey
½ cup peanut oil or other neutral oil
2 tsp sesame oil
2 tsp sesame seeds, lightly toasted
Few drops hot chili oil (optional)

1. Whisk the garlic, ginger, vinegar, soy sauce, and honey together in a bowl or blend them in a mini-food processor. While whisking or with the machine running, pour in the peanut and sesame oils and continue to blend the ingredients until all of the oil is incorporated and the vinaigrette is combined and thickened.
2. Just before serving, stir in the sesame seeds and hot chili oil (if using).
3. The vinaigrette can be prepared up to 3 days in advance. Store it in a covered container in the refrigerator. Shake or whisk the vinaigrette well to recombine it before serving.

APPETIZERS

Gyoza
(Pot Stickers with Roasted Garlic, Mushroom, and Napa Cabbage Filling)

These pot stickers are very easy to fold together. You can make them ahead up to the point of panfrying them; but since they are best hot from the pan, try to cook them at the last possible moment.

MAKES 12 POT STICKERS (4 APPETIZER SERVINGS)

Filling
3 tbsp canola oil, divided
5 shiitake mushrooms, stems removed
Pinch of salt
1 head garlic, roasted and pureed
1 tsp minced garlic
1 tsp lemon zest
1 tsp minced ginger
1½ tsp dark sesame oil
½ cup minced Napa cabbage

Assembly

12 round gyoza wrappers

Water, as needed for brushing wrappers

Drizzle of chili oil

1. To make the filling: Heat 1 tablespoon of oil in a sauté pan over medium heat. Add the shiitake mushrooms, cap side down. Season the mushrooms with a pinch of salt. Cook the first side, pressing down on the mushrooms with a spatula to brown them evenly, about 2 minutes. Turn once and sauté the second side until browned, another 2 minutes.

2. Transfer the shiitake to a cutting board and let them cool before cutting them into small dice. Combine the shiitake with the roasted garlic puree, minced garlic, lemon zest, and 1 teaspoon of the sesame oil with clean hands or a wooden spoon until the ingredients are evenly blended. Add the cabbage and mix thoroughly.

3. To fill the gyoza: Lightly brush the edge of a gyoza wrapper with water. Place about 1 tablespoon of the filling mixture in the center of the wrapper. Fold the wrapper in half, making a half moon. Press the edges of the wrapper together to seal the filling in, and then make 6 pleats along the sealed edge. Pinch each pleat firmly in place. Set the filled gyoza wrapper aside on the prepared baking sheet. Repeat the process until all of the wrappers are filled.

4. The gyoza can be made ahead to this point. Cover them loosely with plastic wrap and keep them refrigerated for up to 12 hours.

5. Heat 2 tablespoons of the canola oil in a large skillet over medium-high heat. Add the gyoza, flat side down, pleated side up. Let them cook undisturbed until the bottoms are a deep brown, about 2 minutes. Carefully pour in the water, and then drizzle the remaining sesame oil over the gyoza. Cover the sauté pan and let the gyoza steam until they are very hot and the wrapper is tender, about 3 minutes.

6. Transfer the gyoza to a heated platter or plates, drizzle them with chili oil, and serve at once.

Beer-Battered Deep-Fried Garlic Cloves

Serve these crispy, nutty garlic cloves on their own as an appetizer accompanied with your favorite marinara sauce for dipping, or use them as a garnish in salads, soups, or stews.

MAKES I POUND

1 cup self-rising flour
½ tsp kosher salt
½ tsp freshly ground black pepper
1 cup beer, room temperature
3 cups vegetable oil, or as needed for frying
1 lb garlic cloves, peeled

1. To make the batter: Whisk the flour, salt, and pepper together in a medium bowl. Add the beer and whisk the batter until it is smooth. The batter can be prepared up to 8 hours in advance. Place the batter in a container, cover it tightly, and keep it in the refrigerator. Stir to recombine the batter before using it to coat the garlic.

2. Preheat a deep fryer to 350°F or heat about 3 inches of oil in a deep, heavy-gauge pot over medium heat. Use a deep-fry thermometer to check the temperature. Another temperature check is to add a 1-inch cube of bread to the oil. It should brown within 30 seconds when the oil is at 350°F.

3. Add about one-fourth of the garlic cloves to the batter and stir to coat them evenly. Lift the garlic out of the batter with a spider or a fork, allowing the excess batter to drain back into the bowl. Lower the coated garlic into the hot oil. Cook the garlic until the batter is puffed and golden brown, about 2 minutes. Lift the fried garlic out of the oil and drain it briefly on paper towels. Keep them warm while frying the remaining garlic.

4. Serve the garlic at once.

Havaadhulee Bis

The name for this dish comes from *havaadhu* (spice or curry) and *bis* (egg). There are no eggs in the recipe; the word *bis* refers to the shape of the dumpling. This version comes from the Indian Ocean island nation of Maldives.

MAKES 6 APPETIZER SERVINGS

Filling

1 (3 oz) can smoked or oil-packed tuna

½ small onion, finely sliced

⅓ cup unsweetened shredded coconut

2 tbsp lime juice

3 curry leaves, finely chopped

3 garlic cloves, minced

1 tsp grated ginger

½ Scotch bonnet chili, seeded and minced (wear gloves)

¼ tsp ground turmeric

Kosher salt, to taste

Dough

2 cups all-purpose flour

1 tsp kosher salt

3 tbsp vegetable oil

¼ cup warm water, plus more as needed

Curry Sauce

2 tbsp vegetable oil

1 onion, finely sliced

2 garlic cloves, finely chopped

1 tsp grated ginger

3 curry leaves, finely sliced

2 tbsp curry powder or paste

1 tbsp chili powder
½ tsp ground cumin
1 tbsp tomato paste
½ cup coconut milk

1. To make the filling: Blend the tuna, onion, coconut, lime juice, curry leaves, garlic, ginger, Scotch bonnet chili, turmeric, and salt. Mash the mixture together with the back of a wooden spoon to make a thick, pasty consistency. Set it aside.

2. To make the dough: Combine the flour and salt in a mixing bowl. Stir in the oil and water and mix to a heavy, stiff dough. Add a little more water, a teaspoonful at a time, if the dough is too dry, but it should not be at all sticky. Divide the dough into pieces about the size of a walnut. Flatten the dough into a round disk.

3. Spoon about 2 teaspoons of the filling mixture into the dough and then wrap the dough completely around the filling. Seal the seams and pinch the ends closed. Roll the filled dough gently between your palms into an oval (egg) shape and set it aside on a lightly floured plate until all the dough has been filled.

4. Bring a large pot of salted water to a boil over high heat. Add the dumplings in batches and cook them, stirring occasionally, until the dough is fully cooked, 6 to 8 minutes. Use a slotted spoon to lift the dumplings into a colander and drain them well. Simmer the remaining dumplings.

5. To make the curry sauce: Heat the oil in a sauté pan over medium-high heat. Add the onion, garlic, ginger, and curry leaves and sauté, stirring frequently, until the onion is tender and translucent, about 4 minutes. Add the curry powder or paste, chili powder, cumin, and tomato paste and stir well to combine. Stir in the coconut milk and bring the sauce to a simmer. Add the dumplings to the curry sauce and simmer until they are very hot, 2 to 3 minutes.

6. Serve at once.

Gambas al Ajillo

This classic Spanish tapas dish features shrimp, plenty of garlic, and a generous splash of brandy. You'll want a few pieces of great bread to sop up the juices in this dish.

MAKES 4 APPETIZER SERVINGS OR 2 MAIN-COURSE SERVINGS

4 oz olive oil
4 garlic cloves, finely minced
1 tsp red pepper flakes
1 lb shrimp, peeled and deveined
¼ cup cognac
1 tbsp lemon juice
1 tsp paprika
Kosher salt and freshly ground black pepper, to taste
1 tbsp chopped fresh parsley

1. Heat the oil in a sauté pan over medium heat. Add the garlic and red pepper flakes and sauté, stirring frequently, until the garlic is fragrant, about 1 minute.
2. Increase the heat to high and immediately add the shrimp, cognac, lemon juice, and paprika. Sauté, stirring frequently, until the shrimp turn pink and the edges curl, about 3 minutes. Season to taste with salt and freshly ground black pepper.
3. Serve the shrimp on heated appetizer plates topped with the pan juices spooned over the shrimp and sprinkled with parsley.

Carciofi alla Giudia
(Artichokes Jewish Style)

Artichokes, flattened and fried in this manner, are considered one of the classics of Roman Jewish cuisine. You can find them in the spring, served by Jewish restaurants in the Roman Ghetto. When properly made, the artichokes look like flowers. A final sprinkle of a few drops of cold water on the hot artichokes gives them their characteristic crispness.

MAKES 4 TO 6 SERVINGS

2 tsp cold water, as needed

2 lemons, juiced

12 baby artichokes

2½ cups extra-virgin olive oil, divided

1 cup chopped fresh flat leaf parsley

10 garlic cloves, minced

½ cup fresh basil leaves

2 tsp sea salt, or to taste

½ tsp freshly ground pepper

Matzo meal, as needed for dredging

1. Combine the water and lemon juice in a bowl. Cut the top ½ inch of the artichoke and trim the barbs from the leaves. Cut the artichokes in half lengthwise, and place them in the lemon water to soak for 30 minutes or until you are ready to fry them.
2. Stir together ½ cup of the olive oil, the parsley, garlic, basil, salt, and pepper in a bowl and set it aside.
3. Heat the remaining 2 cups of olive oil in a deep skillet to 325°F over medium-high heat.
4. Drain the artichokes well, and then hold them by the stems and bang them a little against a work surface to open the leaves. Press

each artichoke on the top to help open out the leaves more. Sprinkle the olive oil-parsley-garlic mixture between the leaves.

5. Place the matzo meal in a shallow dish and roll the artichokes in the meal to coat them evenly. Transfer the artichokes to the hot oil and fry them, turning as necessary to cook evenly, until the artichokes are golden and crisp, about 15 minutes.

6. Blot the artichokes on a paper towel briefly, sprinkle them with a few drops of cold water, and serve at once.

POULTRY

....

Elizabeth David's Lemon and Garlic Marinade for Grilled Cornish Game Hens

The original version of this recipe calls for a very small chicken; this version substitutes game hens that are cut into quarters.

MAKES 4 SERVINGS

12 garlic cloves, separated and peeled

Kosher salt, to taste

3 to 4 tbsp lemon juice

2 tbsp olive oil

2 Cornish game hens (about 1 lb each), backbone removed, quartered

1. Use a mortar and pestle or a knife (see page 122) to mash together the garlic cloves with salt to form a paste. Blend the garlic and lemon juice, then whisk in the olive oil.

2. Place the game hen pieces in a zip-close bag and add the marinade. Seal the bag and turn it to coat the pieces evenly. Marinate the pieces in the refrigerator for at least 8 and up to 24 hours.

3. Preheat a grill to medium-high heat. Remove the game hen from the marinade and scrape away any excess marinade to avoid flare-ups.

4. Grill the game hen over direct heat until it is golden brown on both sides, then move it to indirect heat and cover the grill. Continue to cook the game hen until it is cooked through (165°F).

5. Serve at once.

....

Chicken Vindaloo

Vindaloo originated in the Indian region of Goa and is derived from a Portuguese dish known as *Came de vinha d'alhos,* which means "wine and garlic." The wine has been replaced with vinegar, and this stew is traditionally made with pork and served in Goan Christian homes at Christmas.

MAKES 6 SERVINGS

6 whole red chilies
6 garlic cloves
1 (1 inch) piece ginger
½ cup white wine vinegar
6 boneless skinless chicken breasts, cut into 2-inch cubes
4 tbsp oil
1½ tsp mustard seeds
1 cup diced onions
Dry Spice Mix (recipe follows)
1 tsp brown sugar
½ tsp kosher salt
Chopped cilantro, for garnish

1. Soak the chilies, garlic, and ginger in the white wine vinegar for 30 minutes. Grind the ingredients into a paste in a food processor or in a mortar and pestle. Place the chicken in a zip-close bag and add the

chili paste. Seal the bag and turn it to coat the pieces evenly. Marinate the chicken in the refrigerator for at least 1 and up to 8 hours.

2. Heat the oil in a deep skillet or Dutch oven. Add the mustard seeds and cook them until they start to pop, about 1 minute. Add the onions and sauté, stirring frequently, until golden brown, 5 to 6 minutes. Add the chicken and the chili paste and stir-fry the chicken until it is no longer pink, 2 to 3 minutes. Add the Dry Spice Mix, sugar, and salt and stir to combine.

3. Cover the skillet or Dutch oven and cook over low heat until the chicken is completely cooked, 40 to 45 minutes.

4. Garnish with chopped cilantro and serve at once.

Dry Spice Mix
1 tbsp cumin seeds
1 tsp cloves
1 tsp black peppercorns
1 tsp fenugreek seeds
1 piece (1 inch) cinnamon stick
4 cardamom pods
1 tsp turmeric

1. Put the cumin, cloves, peppercorns, fenugreek, cinnamon, and cardamom in a sauté pan and toast them over medium-high heat, swirling the pan to toast them evenly, until fragrant, about 2 minutes. Transfer the toasted spices to a spice grinder or mortar and pestle. Add the turmeric and grind it all to a powder.

Turkey Satsivi
(Turkey in Georgian Garlic-Walnut Sauce)

This Georgian garlic sauce was a favorite of Georgia's native son, Joseph Stalin, and is a classic dish for gatherings and celebrations throughout the Caucasus region. Ground marigold can be difficult to track down, but you may be able to find it as powdered calendula. Saffron substitutes are also made with marigold, like saffron, because of their rich golden color. Other options include a pinch of turmeric or even saffron.

MAKES 6 TO 8 SERVINGS

1 small (6 to 7 lb) turkey
2 bay leaves
4 sprigs parsley
6 cups water
Walnut Garlic Sauce (recipe follows)

1. Place the turkey in a stockpot and add the bay leaves, parsley, and water. Bring the water to a boil over medium-high heat, cover the pot, and simmer for 45 minutes (the turkey will not be fully cooked, but the broth should be flavorful). Reserve 4 cups of broth for the sauce. Use any remaining broth in soups, sauces, or to cook rice or other grains.

2. Preheat the oven to 350°F. Transfer the turkey to a rack in a roasting pan. Roast the turkey until it is fully cooked (165°F), about 45 minutes. Baste the turkey as it roasts with pan juices. Let the turkey rest for at least 15 minutes before removing the meat from the bones and cutting it into bite-size pieces. Arrange the pieces in a serving dish.

3. While the turkey is roasting, prepare the Walnut-Garlic Sauce.

4. Pour the sauce over the turkey. Allow the Satsivi to cool to room temperature before serving.

Walnut-Garlic Sauce

2 heaping cups shelled walnuts

6 garlic cloves, chopped

4 tbsp butter

3 onions, chopped

1¼ tsp ground cinnamon

1¼ tsp ground marigold

1¼ tsp ground coriander

¾ tsp kosher salt

1¼ tsp freshly ground pepper

½ tsp ground cloves

½ tsp paprika

¼ tsp cayenne

4 cups turkey broth

¼ cup red wine vinegar

1. Grind the walnuts together with the garlic in a food processor until they are chopped fairly fine. Pulse the machine on and off to avoid overgrinding.

2. Add the ground walnuts and garlic to the onions in a skillet and sauté until all the ingredients are evenly blended, about 2 minutes. Return this mixture to the food processor and grind it a second time to make a paste.

3. Return the paste to the skillet and stir in the cinnamon, marigold, coriander, salt, pepper, cloves, paprika, and cayenne. Stir well to combine the ingredients over low heat, about 2 minutes.

4. Gradually stir in the broth reserved from the turkey. Continue to cook the sauce over low heat, stirring occasionally, until it is thick and flavorful, about 20 minutes.

5. Stir in the vinegar.

Galinha à Africana
(African Chicken)

This dish is a fusion of African, European, and Asian flavors that's popular in the former Portuguese colony of Macau. Steamed rice or boiled potatoes are the traditional accompaniment.

MAKES 6 TO 8 SERVINGS

2 tbsp minced shallot

1 tbsp minced garlic

1 tbsp kosher salt

2 tsp five-spice powder

1 tsp chili powder

1 tsp smoked paprika

½ tsp freshly ground black pepper

3 lb chicken pieces

Piri Piri Sauce (recipe follows)

2 tbsp vegetable oil

1. Combine the shallot, garlic, salt, five-spice powder, chili powder, paprika, and black pepper in a small bowl and rub the mix evenly over all surfaces of the chicken. Place the chicken pieces in a container or zip-close bag and marinate them at least 8 and up to 24 hours.

2. While the chicken is marinating, prepare the Piri Piri Sauce.

3. When the chicken is almost finished marinating, preheat the oven to 400°F. Heat the oil in a Dutch oven or flameproof casserole over medium-high heat. Brown the chicken pieces on all sides. (Work in batches so the chicken browns evenly; transfer the chicken to a plate as you finish each batch.)

4. Add the Piri Piri Sauce to the Dutch oven or casserole and stir well to dissolve any meat drippings in the pan. Return the chicken pieces to the sauce and turn them to coat each piece evenly. Bake the chicken until it is cooked through (165°F), about 30 minutes.

Piri Piri Sauce

¼ cup vegetable oil

1 cup minced shallot

½ cup minced garlic

½ cup grated fresh coconut

½ cup sweet paprika

1 tsp chili powder

1 cup chicken broth or water

½ cup coconut milk

2 tbsp peanut butter

2 bay leaves

Kosher salt, to taste

1. Heat the oil in a saucepan over medium-low heat. Add the shallots and garlic and sauté, stirring frequently, until they are tender and translucent, about 5 minutes. Add the coconut, chili powder, and paprika and stir until the sauce is evenly blended, about 2 minutes.
2. Stir in the broth or water, coconut milk, peanut butter, and bay leaves. Stir until the sauce is smooth. Simmer the sauce over low heat until it is flavorful and lightly thickened, about 10 minutes. Remove and discard the bay leaves.

....

Chicken Ghiveci

This braised chicken dish is popular in Romania and Moldova. Serve it with plenty of good bread to sop up the sauce.

MAKES 4 TO 6 SERVINGS

3 tbsp olive oil

2½ lb chicken pieces, or cut-ups

1 medium onion, thinly sliced

5 garlic cloves, minced

2 red bell peppers, cut into strips

½ cup tomato paste

½ cup dry white wine

2 large potatoes, cubed

2 carrots, sliced into ½-inch-thick rounds

1 pinch dried thyme

1 pinch dried rosemary

1 pinch sugar

1 pinch kosher salt

1 pinch pepper

1. Heat the oil in a Dutch oven or flameproof casserole over medium-low heat. Add the chicken pieces, working in batches, and cook them on all sides until they are golden, about 5 minutes. Transfer them to a plate.

2. Add the onion and garlic to the Dutch oven or casserole and sauté, stirring frequently, until they are tender and translucent, about 3 minutes. Add the peppers and sauté, stirring frequently, until tender, about 3 minutes. Stir in the tomato paste until it is blended into the vegetables, about 2 minutes. Add the wine, and then stir in the potatoes, carrots, thyme, rosemary, sugar, salt, and pepper.

3. Return the chicken pieces and cover the Dutch oven or casserole. Cook it over low heat until the chicken is cooked through (165°F) and the potatoes and carrots are tender, 40 to 45 minutes. Serve at once in heated bowls.

Muamba de Galinha

This spicy Angolan chicken dish is usually made with red palm oil. Those who are unaccustomed may find palm oil's very strong taste objectionable, so this recipe suggests olive oil instead. If you have access to red palm oil, however, try it at least once for the authentic experience. Serve this dish accompanied with steamed rice to help tame the bite from the cayenne peppers.

2½ lb chicken pieces (breasts, thighs, drumsticks)
Kosher salt and freshly ground pepper, to taste
1 (2 lb) Delicata squash (or substitute 2 cups cubed pumpkin or
   butternut squash)
4 tbsp olive oil or red palm oil
2 onions, sliced
8 garlic cloves, minced
2 cayenne peppers, seeded and sliced
1 cup chicken broth
3 Roma tomatoes, quartered
¼ tsp grains of paradise (or substitute ¼ tsp ground cardamom
   and ¼ tsp ground black pepper)
1 bay leaf
Kosher salt and freshly ground black pepper, to taste

1. Preheat the oven to 350°F. Place the chicken pieces in a baking dish, season them with salt and pepper, and bake the chicken until it is cooked through (165°F), about 40 minutes. Reserve the chicken and any pan juices to add to the stew.

2. Roast the squash while the chicken is roasting. Place the squash in a baking dish, pierce it in two or three places with a skewer or the tip of a knife. Bake the squash until it is very tender, about 30 minutes. (If using cubed pumpkin or butternut squash, bake it in a covered dish for 15 to 20 minutes.)

3. Heat the olive oil or red palm oil in a Dutch oven or flameproof casserole over medium heat. Add the onions, garlic, and cayenne pepper and sauté, stirring frequently, until the onions are tender and translucent, about 6 minutes.

4. Add the reserved chicken pieces with pan juices and the squash. Add the chicken broth, tomatoes, grains of paradise, bay leaf, salt, and pepper. Cover and cook for about 20 to 30 minutes. Remove and discard the bay leaf.

5. Serve at once in a heated serving dish or plates.

Poule au Pot

Henri IV, who was baptized with garlic and known to eat prodigious quantities of it, was also known for promising his people "a chicken in every pot." This dish is a garlicky version of Henri IV's promise. Free-range chickens have a more pronounced flavor, essential to the success of this dish.

MAKES 4 TO 6 SERVINGS

4 sweet potatoes, cut into wedges

4 carrots, cut into 1-inch-thick rounds

4 celery stalks, cut into 1-inch-thick pieces

4 leeks, white and light green portion only, chopped

1 (3 lb) chicken

2 slices pancetta, minced (optional)

1 large head garlic, cloves separated but not peeled, divided

2 lemons, quartered, divided

8 sprigs parsley, divided

6 sprigs thyme, divided

2 sprigs rosemary, divided

Kosher salt and freshly ground black pepper, as needed

2 tbsp olive oil

½ cup dry white wine

1 cup chicken broth

1. Preheat the oven to 325°F.
2. Place the sweet potatoes, carrots, and celery in a baking dish to make a bed for the chicken. Scatter the vegetables evenly with the leeks.
3. Stuff the chicken with the pancetta (if using) and half of the garlic, lemons, parsley, thyme, and rosemary. Season it with salt and pepper. Place the chicken on the vegetable bed and scatter the remaining garlic, lemon, parsley, thyme, and rosemary around the chicken.

Drizzle the oil over the chicken, add the wine and broth, cover loosely, and bake the chicken until it is cooked through (165°F), 2 to 2½ hours.

4. Let the chicken rest at least 10 minutes before carving it into portions.

5. Remove and discard the herb sprigs and lemon wedges from the vegetable mixture. Spoon the vegetables and the broth into heated soup plates. Top with the chicken and serve at once.

Poulet Béarnaise

In *Provence,* Ford Madox Ford's rapturous ode to the region, the author describes a recipe given to him by a glamorous young woman from London, reputed to be one of the best chefs in the city. The recipe she shared was this one, Poulet Béarnaise—chicken roasted over two pounds of blanched garlic. If you can trust your guests not to swallow the garlic skin, you don't really have to peel them, although blanching them first does make the task easier.

MAKES 6 TO 8 SERVINGS

1 (4 to 5 lb) chicken
Kosher salt and freshly ground black pepper, to taste
½ cup olive oil, more if needed
2 lb garlic cloves (about 14 heads), blanched and peeled, divided
4 large baking potatoes, peeled and cut into wedges

1. Preheat the oven to 325°F. Truss the chicken (see Note) and season it all over with salt and pepper.

2. Heat the oil in a large sauté pan over medium heat. Brown the chicken in the oil, turning it to cook it evenly on all sides, about 20 minutes. Transfer the chicken to a plate; stuff the cavity with about one-fourth of the blanched garlic.

3. Return the pan to medium heat and add more oil if necessary. Add the remaining garlic cloves and stir them to coat each evenly with olive oil. Transfer the garlic to a baking dish to make an even bed. Set the chicken on top of the garlic.

4. Return the pan to medium-high heat and add more oil if necessary. Add the potatoes and brown them lightly on all sides, turning as necessary. Transfer the potatoes to the baking dish around the chicken. Cover the baking dish and bake the chicken until it is cooked through (165°F), about 1½ hours.

5. Let the chicken rest for about 15 minutes before carving it into pieces to serve. Accompany the chicken with the potatoes and garlic, and spoon the pan juices over each serving.

NOTE

The point of trussing a bird is to hold the ends of the drumstick in. By trussing the chicken, the meat cooks more evenly and is less likely to dry out. The technique is like lacing a sneaker. Cut a 2-foot length of butcher's string. Run the string underneath the wings and cross one end over the other on the back of the chicken. Pull the string taut and even out the ends, so they are about the same length. Run the string down along the side of the breast. Pull the string up around the ends of each drumstick. Pull the string tight and tie it securely.

LAMB

~~~~

Simca's Lamb Stew Provençal with 140 Cloves of Garlic

Simone Beck, aka Simca, was one of Julia Child's co-authors on both volumes of *Mastering the Art of French Cooking*. This recipe is known as a *pistache* because the garlic is cooked long enough to acquire a nutty flavor. It calls for a parchment lid, also known as a cartouche; just cut a piece of parchment into a round the same diameter as your casserole or Dutch oven. Beck recommends green beans sautéed in butter as an accompaniment.

MAKES 6 TO 8 SERVINGS

4 to 5 tbsp olive oil

3 lb boneless lamb shoulder, cut into 3-inch pieces

2½ tbsp herbes de Provence

1 tsp kosher salt

½ tsp freshly ground black pepper

1½ cups dry white wine

140 garlic cloves (about 5 heads), unpeeled

1½ cups chicken or beef broth, divided

4 tbsp butter

2 tbsp finely minced fresh parsley, for garnish

1. Preheat the oven to 300°F.
2. Heat the olive oil in a large sauté pan over medium heat. Add the lamb in an even layer. Brown the lamb evenly on all sides, turning it as necessary, about 10 minutes.
3. Scatter the herbes de Provence, salt, and pepper evenly over the lamb. Add the wine and bring it to a simmer, allowing it to bubble before adding the unpeeled garlic cloves and ½ cup of the broth.
4. Press a round of parchment paper (cartouche) onto the surface of the stew, and then cover the Dutch oven or casserole with a lid. Braise the lamb in the oven until the meat is tender but not stringy, about 2 hours. Add the broth in ½ cup increments while the stew cooks to keep the meat moist.
5. Strain the stew through a sieve, catching the liquid in a clean saucepan, and skim away any fat from the surface. Separate the lamb from the garlic and set the lamb aside. Push the garlic through a sieve with the back of a spoon directly into the liquid from the stew. Simmer the liquid and garlic together until it is lightly thickened, about 4 minutes. Stir in the butter, and then return the lamb to the sauce, turning the meat to coat it evenly, and reheat.
6. Serve the stew in heated soup plates sprinkled with parsley.

....

Plov with Lamb

Plov is Uzbekistan's native dish. It includes one head of garlic per person, served whole for each person to eat along with the pilaf. For a traditional flavor, replace the oil with rendered lamb fat.

MAKES 4 TO 6 SERVINGS

3 tbsp olive oil or rendered lamb fat
2 lb boneless lamb leg, cut into 1-inch cubes
2 onions, sliced
4 carrots, coarsely shredded
1 tsp ground cumin

1 tsp kosher salt

1 tsp red pepper flakes

2 cups long-grain rice

3½ cups water

4 to 6 heads garlic

¼ cup slivered dried apricots, for garnish (optional)

1. Heat the oil or lamb fat in a Dutch oven or flameproof casserole over medium-high heat. Add the lamb and cook it in batches, turning it as necessary until it is evenly browned on all sides, about 5 minutes. Transfer it to a plate and set it aside.

2. Add the onions to the pan and sauté them over medium heat, stirring frequently, until they are golden brown, about 10 minutes. Add the carrots and sauté them until they are tender, about 3 minutes. Return the meat and any juices it may have released to the pan, and season it with the cumin, salt, and red pepper flakes. Sprinkle the rice in an even layer over the meat. Pour in the water around the edges of the pan to avoid disturbing the layers. Tuck the garlic heads into the stew. Cover the Dutch oven or casserole, place it in the oven, and cook the dish until the rice is tender and has absorbed all the liquid, 20 to 25 minutes.

3. Fold the apricot (if using) into the pilaf. Serve at once in heated bowls and accompany each portion with a head of garlic.

Xinjiang Lamb and Chili Kebabs

In Western China, these mouth-numbingly spicy skewers are standard fare at Kinjiang restaurants—hole-in-the-wall places—where you'll find them piled upon the table while the bar offers beer and rice whiskey to drink. The authentic version calls for bits of tail fat to be sandwiched between the meat before cooking. It melts onto the lamb for an intense flavor. Elsewhere, the shoulder cut is considered best for this addictive dish, since it is the fattiest cut of meat. Once grilled, the combination of lamb with garlic and spices is hard to resist.

MAKES 3 TO 4 SERVINGS

1½ lb boneless lamb shoulder
2 tbsp cumin seeds
2 tbsp coriander seeds
6 garlic cloves, minced
2 tbsp chili flakes
2 tsp kosher salt

1. Trim any silver skin or tendons from the meat but leave on the fat. Cut the meat in long, thin strips against the grain; the meat should be about ¼ inch thick.
2. Toast the cumin and coriander seeds in a small, dry sauté pan over medium heat, swirling or stirring the spices frequently, until fragrant, about 2 minutes. Grind the spices into a coarse powder in a spice grinder or mortar and pestle.
3. Combine these spices with the garlic, chili flakes, and salt in a bowl or a zip-close bag. Add the lamb, tossing it until it is coated evenly and lightly massaging the rub into the lamb. Cover and refrigerate the meat at least 6 and up to 24 hours.
4. Preheat a gas or charcoal grill to medium-high heat. Soak wooden skewers in cold water for 10 minutes before threading the lamb pieces on the skewers; do not pack the lamb too tightly.

5. Grill the skewers, turning them as necessary, until they are well browned and the doneness you prefer, about 8 minutes for medium. Let the lamb rest for about 10 minutes before serving.

....

Massaman Lamb Curry

This Thai curry is served in a curry-coconut sauce of Muslim (Massaman) origin. It's great over jasmine rice.

MAKES 4 TO 6 SERVINGS

2½ cups chicken or beef broth

2 lb lamb shoulder, cut into cubes or pieces

⅓ cup diced onion

3 bay leaves

1 (3 inch) piece ginger, grated

5 garlic cloves, minced

1 stalk lemongrass, tender inner portion minced

¼ cup chopped, unsalted cashews, plus a few whole
    nuts for garnish

2 tbsp fish sauce

2 tsp tamarind paste

¾ tsp red pepper flakes

1 tsp ground coriander

1 tsp ground cumin

1 tsp ground turmeric

1 tsp brown sugar

½ tsp white pepper

⅛ tsp ground cardamom

14 oz coconut milk

1 large potato, cut into chunks

½ cup green beans

¼ cup finely shredded fresh basil, plus more for garnish

1. Bring the broth to a boil in a large pot over high heat. Add the lamb, onion, and bay leaves, and return the broth to a boil. Reduce the heat to low, cover the pot, and simmer, stirring occasionally, until the meat is tender, about 40 minutes.
2. Add the ginger, garlic, lemongrass, cashews, fish sauce, tamarind paste, red pepper flakes, coriander, cumin, turmeric, sugar, pepper, and cardamom and stir well to combine. Stir in the coconut milk, potatoes, and green beans. Simmer over medium-low heat, stirring occasionally, until the potatoes are tender, about 30 minutes.
3. Just before serving, stir in the basil.
4. Transfer to a serving bowl, or plate up on individual plates or bowls. Top with a few more cashews and fresh basil.

BEEF

Knockwurst with Ale and Sauerkraut

Knockwurst, made from beef, pork, and a lot of garlic, have been popular since the fourteenth century and were believed to be a favorite of the royal House of Hapsburg. Today, served with sauerkraut and a stein of *bier*, knockwurst is the centerpiece of Germany's legendary Oktoberfest.

MAKES 8 SERVINGS

8 knockwurst
2 garlic cloves, crushed
1 (12 oz) bottle ale
1 tbsp olive oil
1 lb prepared sauerkraut
8 hot dog buns
4 tbsp spicy brown mustard
1 tsp freshly ground black pepper

1. Pierce the knockwurst in 2 or 3 places with a fork and place it in a

dish. Add the crushed garlic and ale. Cover and marinate the knock-wurst in the refrigerator for at least 1 and up to 6 hours.

2. Preheat a broiler to high.

3. Heat oil in a cast-iron skillet over medium-high heat. Add sauer-kraut and sauté, stirring frequently, until very hot. Spread the sauerkraut in an even layer and put the knockwurst on top. Pour the ale-and-garlic marinade over the knockwurst. Cover the skil-let and transfer it to the oven. Bake the knockwurst until it is very hot, about 10 minutes. Remove the cover and continue baking the knockwurst until it is lightly browned on the top.

4. Transfer the knockwurst to the hot dog buns. Stir the mustard and pepper into the sauerkraut, and spoon the sauerkraut over the knockwurst. Serve at once.

Braised Brisket with 36 Cloves of Garlic

Braises are almost invariably better the day after they are cooked, so if you have enough advance time, follow the note at the end of this recipe for cooling the brisket and sauce. Not only do the flavor and texture improve, but it is also easier to slice the beef when it is cold.

MAKES 8 SERVINGS

3 lb beef brisket
Kosher salt and freshly ground pepper, to taste
3 tbsp olive oil
3 heads garlic, cloves blanched and peeled
2 tbsp red wine vinegar
3 cups beef or chicken broth
4 sprigs thyme
2 sprigs rosemary plus 1 tsp chopped leaves
1 tsp minced garlic
1 tsp grated lemon zest

1. Preheat the oven to 325°F.

2. Pat the brisket dry and season it generously with salt and pepper on all sides.

3. Heat the olive oil in a Dutch oven or flameproof casserole over medium-high heat. Use two burners, if necessary. Brown the brisket about 5 minutes on each side. Transfer the brisket to a platter and set it aside.

4. Pour off all but about 1 tablespoon of fat from the pan and add the garlic cloves. Cook them over medium heat, stirring occasionally, until the garlic is just starting to turn a golden brown. Add the vinegar and stir well to dissolve the meat drippings. Add the broth, thyme, and rosemary sprigs and reduce the heat to a simmer. Return the brisket to the pan, fat side up. Spoon some of the garlic cloves on top of the beef.

5. Cover the Dutch oven or casserole and braise, basting the top of the beef every half hour, until the meat is fork tender, 2½ to 3 hours. If the liquid in the pan begins to bubble or boil, set the cover slightly ajar and turn the oven down to 300°F. Transfer the brisket to a platter and moisten it with a ladleful of the cooking liquid.

6. To finish the sauce, put the Dutch oven or casserole over medium-high heat and bring it to a simmer. Remove and discard the thyme and rosemary sprigs. Skim as much fat as possible from the surface. Use a potato masher or the back of a wooden spoon to mash the garlic into the sauce for a rustic sauce (see the Note below for making a smoother sauce). Add the chopped rosemary, minced garlic, and lemon zest. Simmer this sauce over medium-high heat until it is lightly thickened, about 4 minutes. Season with salt and pepper.

7. Slice the brisket about ½ inch thick across the grain and arrange the slices in an ovenproof serving platter. Spoon the sauce over the beef and return it to the oven until the beef is very hot, about 10 minutes.

If you are preparing this dish a day in advance, cool the brisket and pan sauce to room temperature, then cover it well and refrigerate overnight. The next day, lift off all solid fat from the surface. Remove the brisket from the pan and slice it thinly across the grain. Finish the sauce as described above and bake the brisket and sauce together in a 325°F, covered, until very hot, about 20 to 25 minutes.

To make a smoother sauce, strain the garlic from the sauce, catching the broth in a clean saucepan, and puree it in a food processor along with about 1 cup of the broth. Return this puree to the remaining broth and finish the sauce with rosemary, garlic, and lemon.

Beef Tenderloin with Mustard-Garlic-Herb Crust

This festive creation is ideal for a holiday centerpiece, and it is incredibly easy to prepare and serve. The Garlic-Horseradish Sauce makes the dish unforgettable.

MAKES 4 TO 6 SERVINGS

1 (2½ lb) piece beef tenderloin, trimmed
Kosher salt and freshly ground black pepper, to taste
2 tbsp olive oil
⅓ cup whole-grain mustard
6 garlic cloves, minced
2 tbsp fresh thyme leaves
2 tbsp fresh rosemary, finely chopped
1 tsp balsamic vinegar

1. Preheat the oven to 375°F
2. Season the beef tenderloin with salt and pepper. Heat the oil in a large skillet over medium-high heat. Add the tenderloin and sear it on all sides until it is evenly browned, about 8 minutes. Transfer the beef to a rack in a roasting pan.

3. To make the crust: Stir together the mustard, garlic, thyme, rosemary, and balsamic vinegar. Rub the mixture evenly over the roast, covering the top and sides.
4. Roast the meat until a meat thermometer registers 125°F for rare, about 30 minutes. Let the tenderloin rest for about 10 minutes before carving it into slices.
5. Serve with the Garlic-Horseradish Sauce (recipe follows).

Garlic-Horseradish Sauce
MAKES 1 CUP

2 cups heavy cream
1 head garlic, roasted and pureed
¼ cup drained bottled horseradish
Kosher sat and white pepper, to taste

Simmer the cream in a heavy saucepan over low heat, stirring occasionally, until reduced by about half, 20 to 25 minutes. Stir in the garlic and horseradish. Season to taste with salt and pepper.

....

Vietnamese-Style Beef with Garlic, Black Pepper, and Lime

Garlic and pepper are a great match for each other, each lending its own particular brand of heat.

MAKES 4 SERVINGS

2 tbsp soy sauce
2 tbsp lime juice
1½ tbsp light brown sugar
1 tbsp fish sauce
5 garlic cloves, minced
2 tsp peanut or canola oil, plus 2 tbsp for stir-frying
½ tsp freshly ground black pepper, plus more as needed

1 ½ lb beef tri-tip steak or tenderloin, cut into ¼-inch-thick strips
Kosher salt, as needed
1 medium yellow onion, sliced lengthwise, ¼ inch thick
3 tbsp chopped dry-roasted peanuts, for garnish
2 scallions, green and white parts, thinly sliced, for garnish

1. Stir together the soy sauce, lime juice, sugar, and fish sauce in a small bowl until the sugar dissolves. In another small bowl, stir together the garlic, 2 teaspoons of the oil, and ½ teaspoon of the black pepper.
2. Season the beef with salt and pepper. Heat 1 tablespoon of the oil in a wok or a large skillet. Working in batches, add the beef strips in a single layer and cook them on the first side until browned, about 1 minute. Turn the strips once and cook them on the second side, about 1 minute. Transfer the strips to a plate and set them aside. Let the wok or skillet reheat before adding more beef. Add more oil as necessary.
3. Return the wok to high heat and heat 1 tablespoon oil. Add the onion and stir-fry until it is softened and translucent, 2 to 3 minutes. Add the garlic-oil-pepper mixture and stir-fry until the mixture is fragrant, 30 seconds. Add the soy sauce mixture and continue to stir-fry until the beef and onions are tender and well coated with the sauce, 2 to 3 minutes.
4. Serve at once, garnished with peanuts and scallions.

PORK

Pork Adobo

This entrée is considered the national dish of the Philippines. If you like, you can tie the peppercorns up in a piece of cheesecloth or put them in a tea ball so you can remove them from the dish. If you don't mind the punch of eating an occasional peppercorn with the pork, you can skip that step.

MAKES 4 SERVINGS

1½ lb pork tenderloin, cut into bite-size pieces

24 garlic cloves, minced

⅓ cup apple cider vinegar

3 tbsp soy sauce

1 tbsp black peppercorns

2 bay leaves

½ cup water

1 tbsp vegetable oil

1. Combine the pork tenderloin with one-third of the garlic, the vinegar, soy sauce, peppercorns, and the bay leaves in a pot. Let the pork marinate in the refrigerator for at least 1 and up to 8 hours.

2. Place the pot over medium heat and bring it to a boil. Add the water, cover the pot, and simmer it over low heat until the pork is very tender. Use a slotted spoon to lift the pork from the sauce in the pan. Remove and discard the bay leaves.

3. Heat a skillet over medium-high heat. Add the oil and the remaining garlic. Sauté, stirring constantly, until the garlic is golden, about 1 minute. Add the pork to the garlic and sauté until hot, about 2 minutes. Add the sauce to the pork and bring it to a simmer, 2 minutes. Serve at once in heated soup plates.

....

Moo Gratium

This delicious Thai-fried garlic pork dish is quick and easy to prepare.

MAKES 4 TO 6 SERVINGS

1 lb pork tenderloin, trimmed

4 tbsp garlic, minced

4 tbsp soy sauce

1 tsp freshly ground black pepper

1 tsp sugar

2 tbsp neutral oil (canola or vegetable)

4 cups steamed jasmine rice

1 cucumber, thinly sliced, for garnish

6 sprigs cilantro, for garnish

4 eggs, fried (optional)

1. Cut the pork into thin 1-inch-wide strips. Combine the pork with the garlic, soy sauce, pepper, and sugar in a bowl or a zip-close bag. Toss the pork to coat it evenly and marinate it in the refrigerator for at least 30 minutes and up to 4 hours.

2. Heat the oil in a wok or sauté pan over medium-high heat. Add the marinated pork and all the marinade to the oil and stir-fry the pork until it is cooked through, about 5 minutes.

3. Serve at once with jasmine rice and garnish with cucumbers and cilantro. Top each portion with a fried egg (if using).

....

Mojo Criollo Pulled Pork

This Cuban pulled pork is marinated in and served with *mojo criollo,* a citrus-garlic sauce. The traditional accompaniment is rice and black beans.

MAKES 8 TO 10 SERVINGS

1 (5 lb) bone-in pork shoulder
6 garlic cloves, thinly sliced
2 tsp ground cumin
½ tsp freshly ground black pepper
2 cups Mojo Criollo Sauce (recipe follows), plus extra to garnish
¼ cup water
2 yellow onions, sliced into ¼-inch-thick rounds
1 tbsp olive oil
2 tbsp chopped cilantro
Kosher salt and freshly ground black pepper, as needed

1. Make the Mojo Criollo Sauce (recipe follows).

2. Cut small slits evenly over the surface of the pork and slide a garlic slice into each once. Sprinkle the pork with cumin and black pepper, place it in a large zip-close bag, and pour in 1 cup of the Mojo Criollo Sauce (recipe follows). Marinate the meat in the refrigerator, turning it every hour, for at least 3 and up to 8 hours.

3. Preheat the oven to 325°F. Place the pork in a Dutch oven. Add ¼ cup of the Mojo Criollo Sauce and water. Cover the Dutch oven and place it in the oven. Every hour, check the roast and add a bit more

water if the pan is too dry. Roast until the pork is fork tender and can easily be pulled apart, 4 to 5 hours. Remove pork from the oven and let it stand, uncovered, for 20 minutes.

4. Separate the onion slices into rings and place them in a shallow dish. Cover them with the remaining ¾ cup of the Mojo Criollo Sauce. Heat the olive oil in a sauté pan over medium-high heat. Add the sauce and onions and cook, stirring frequently, until the onions are tender and translucent, about 6 minutes.

5. Using two forks, shred the pork roast and place it on a serving platter. Drizzle Mojo Criollo Sauce over the pork and top it with the onions. Sprinkle the dish with the cilantro, season it with salt and pepper, and serve at once.

Mojo Criollo Sauce
12 garlic cloves, mashed to a paste with 1 tbsp salt
1 cup water
½ cup lime juice
½ cup orange juice
2 tbsp dried oregano
2 bay leaves
1 tsp ground cumin

Combine the garlic paste, water, lime juice, orange juice, oregano, bay leaves, and cumin. Let this sauce rest in the refrigerator for at least 1 hour or overnight.

SEAFOOD

~~~~~~

Bouillabaisse

Bouillabaisse is French for boil (*bouille*) and reduce (*abaisse*). This legendary seafood melange, originally from the port city of Marseilles, is served with a garlicky rouille.

MAKES 6 SERVINGS

Croutons

12 baguette slices, ½ inch thick

2 garlic cloves, peeled and halved

½ cup extra-virgin olive oil

2 yellow onions, thinly sliced

5 garlic cloves, minced

¼ cup chopped fennel tops

3 sprigs parsley

3 sprigs thyme

1 bay leaf

1 lb fingerling potatoes, scrubbed

1½ lb plum tomatoes, peeled, seeded, and chopped

4 lb cleaned assorted fish and seafood (red snapper, sea bass, tile-
fish, grouper, striped bass, monkfish, halibut, cuttlefish, tilapia,
squid), cut into chunks if necessary
16 mussels, scrubbed and de-bearded
10 cups fish broth, warm
1 tsp crumbled saffron threads
½ cup Pernod
Kosher salt and freshly ground black pepper, as needed
1 cup Rouille (recipe follows)

1. Preheat the oven to 350°F. Place the baguette slices on a cookie
   sheet and toast the slices until they are golden and crisp, about 10
   minutes. While the toasted slices are still warm, rub them with the
   halved garlic. Set them aside.
2. Pour ¼ cup of the oil into a large, deep pot over medium-high heat.
   Add the onions, minced garlic, fennel tops, parsley, thyme, and bay
   leaf and sauté until the onions are tender and translucent, about
   5 minutes. Layer the potatoes and then the tomatoes over the onions. Add the fish and seafood and the mussels. Pour in the fish
   broth and then the remaining ¼ cup of oil. Add saffron and Pernod,
   season the broth with salt and pepper, and bring it to a boil over
   high heat. Remove the seafood as it cooks, transferring it to a platter. The mussels are usually open after 8 to 10 minutes, the more
   delicate varieties of fish and seafood will take about 12 minutes, and
   the potatoes will take about 20 minutes.
3. Strain the broth and serve it as a first course accompanied with garlic croutons spread with Rouille. Serve the fish and potatoes as the
   second course.

Rouille

No bouillabaisse is authentic without this garlicky Provençal paste (the
name means "rust" in French, a reference to its color).

1 pinch saffron threads, crumbled

2 tbsp fish or clam broth

4 garlic cloves, peeled and minced

1 cup prepared mayonnaise

½ tsp sweet paprika

Pinch ground cayenne

Kosher salt

Combine the saffron and broth in a food processor or mortar and pestle. Add the garlic and puree or crush until smooth. Transfer the mixture to a bowl and stir in the mayonnaise, paprika, and cayenne. Season it to taste with salt. Rouille is best used the same day it is made.

....

Grand Aioli

There are no absolute rules concerning what you should serve as part of a grand aioli. You can serve a simple dish of boiled potatoes, or you can make it much more elaborate with a variety of fish, seafood, and vegetables. See the Note following this recipe for some suggestions.

MAKES 2 CUPS

2 large egg yolks, room temperature

8 garlic cloves, minced

Pinch kosher salt

¾ cup extra-virgin olive oil

4 tsp lemon juice, plus more as needed

1 tsp Dijon mustard

¾ cup peanut oil

Kosher salt and freshly ground black pepper, to taste

1. To make the aioli by hand: Put the egg yolks in a medium bowl. Add the garlic and a pinch of salt; whisk the ingredients to combine

them. While whisking, add the olive oil a few drops at a time until all of the oil is blended into the egg yolk. Whisk in the lemon juice and mustard, and then continue, adding the peanut oil while whisking, a little at a time, until all of the oil is blended into the sauce. Adjust the seasoning with lemon juice, salt, and pepper.

2. To make the aioli in a blender: Add the egg yolks and garlic to the pitcher of the blender. Puree for a few seconds to combine the ingredients. Add a pinch of salt, and then, with the blender running, pour the oil through the opening in the lid until you have added all of the olive oil. Add the lemon juice and mustard with the machine running, and then gradually add the peanut oil until it has all been blended into the sauce. Adjust the seasoning with lemon juice, salt, and pepper.

3. Serve with a selection of grilled, poached, and steamed fish and/or vegetables.

NOTE

Plan on about 6 to 8 ounces of fish for each person and about 1 cup of steamed vegetables. Here are a few suggestions.

Grilled tuna
Poached salmon, halibut, or cod
Steamed asparagus, broccoli, or cauliflower
Marinated artichoke hearts or bottoms
Grilled zucchini or yellow squash
Steamed or boiled new potatoes
Hard-cooked eggs

Blaff

Fish marinated in lime juice and garlic is a traditional preparation on the Caribbean island of Martinique.

MAKES 6 SERVINGS

2 lb red snapper fish fillets or other firm white fish
4 cups water
½ cup lime juice
4 scallions, chopped
2 Scotch bonnet peppers or other hot chili pepper, minced
4 garlic cloves, minced
1 tsp kosher salt
3 cups steamed long-grain rice
Lime wedges, to serve

1. Combine the fish, 2 cups of the water, lime juice, scallions, Scotch bonnet peppers, garlic, and salt in a large container. Cover and marinate the fish in the refrigerator for at least 1 and up to 12 hours.
2. Remove the fish from the marinade and set it aside. Combine the marinade with the remaining 2 cups of water in a saucepan and bring it to a boil over medium-high heat. Simmer over medium-low heat until the broth is flavorful and slightly reduced, about 5 minutes.
3. Add the fish to the simmering broth and simmer for another 10 minutes, or until the fish is cooked through and flakes easily. Taste the broth and adjust the seasoning with salt and pepper if necessary.
4. To serve, divide the rice evenly among 6 heated soup plates. Top the rice with the fish and then a ladle of the broth. Serve at once with lime wedges.

Bukharian Fried Fish with Cilantro-Garlic Sauce

This is a traditional Jewish Sabbath dinner in Bukhara, Uzbekistan. As Bukhara is landlocked, the dish is usually prepared with freshwater fish like trout, pike, or catfish.

MAKES 4 TO 6 SERVINGS

5 garlic cloves, peeled
2 tsp kosher salt
1 cup water
1 cup finely chopped cilantro leaves
2 lb firm-fleshed fish fillets or steaks
Vegetable oil, as needed for frying

1. Make a garlic-cilantro sauce by combining the garlic, 1 teaspoon of the salt, ½ cup of the water, and cilantro in a food processor and process the ingredients to a fine puree. Season the sauce with additional salt if necessary and set it aside.

2. Arrange the fish fillets or steaks in a single layer in a deep platter or pan. Dissolve 1 teaspoon of salt in the remaining ½ cup of water to make a brine and pour it over the fish. Refrigerate the fish in the brine for about 20 minutes. Drain the brine from the fish and pat the fillets completely dry with paper towels.

3. Heat ¼ inch of oil in a large, heavy skillet over medium heat until it shimmers. Add the fish and fry, turning the fillets once, until golden brown, about 10 minutes. Blot the fish briefly on paper towels, and then transfer to a serving platter or individual plates. Top the fish with the garlic-cilantro sauce and serve at room temperature or chilled.

Singapore Chili Garlic Shrimp

The cuisine of Singapore is a blend of cultures and flavors. This dish reflects Chinese, Indian, and even some Vietnamese flavors. Whether or not chili shrimp is the most popular of all Singaporean dishes, it is certainly one of them. You can find active debates about which street stands sell the best version of this dish; but in the meantime, try it for yourself with shrimp or substitute the equally traditional crab.

MAKES 4 SERVINGS

6 tbsp soy sauce

6 tbsp water

¼ cup rice vinegar

4 tsp dark sesame oil

¼ cup ketchup

2 tbsp sugar

2 tbsp cornstarch

3 tbsp corn oil

1½ lb jumbo shrimp (16–20 count)

2 tbsp ginger

4 garlic cloves, minced

1 jalapeño chili, minced

6 scallions, thinly sliced

4 cups steamed long-grain white rice

1. Combine the soy sauce, water, vinegar, sesame oil, ketchup, sugar, and cornstarch in a bowl and stir until the sugar and cornstarch are dissolved. Set this sauce aside.
2. Heat 2 tablespoons of corn oil in a wok or sauté pan over high heat. Add the shrimp and stir-fry the shrimp until it is seared on both sides, about 1 minute on each side.
3. Transfer the shrimp to a bowl. Return the wok or sauté pan to high heat and add the remaining 1 tablespoon of oil. Add the ginger, garlic,

chili, and about two-thirds of the scallions and stir-fry until fragrant, about 10 seconds.

4. Return the shrimp to the wok or sauté pan and stir-fry until they are cooked through and the sauce has thickened slightly, about 1 minute.

5. Serve the shrimp on a heated platter with the sauce and garnished with the remaining scallions, accompanied with the rice.

....

Lasooni Jhiinga
(Indian Garlic Shrimp)

The name of this dish, said to have originated in Rajasthan in India, is a little lesson in Indian vocabulary: *lasooni* means "garlic"; *jhinga* is "shrimp"; and *kadai,* the sauce featured in this dish, means "wok." Be sure to leave enough time for the shrimp to marinate in the spice and chili paste.

MAKES 4 SERVINGS

½ tsp kosher salt
½ tsp turmeric
½ tsp chili powder
16 large shrimp, peeled and deveined
2 tbsp oil
5 or 6 garlic cloves, minced
1 green chili, julienned
1 red chili, julienned
7 tbsp Kadai Sauce (recipe follows)
1 scallion, julienned
½ lemon, juiced
Kosher salt, to taste

1. Combine the salt, turmeric, and chili powder and rub it evenly into the shrimp. Let the shrimp marinate in the refrigerator for at least 30 minutes and up to 8 hours.

2. Heat the oil in a wok or sauté pan. Add the garlic and stir-fry the gar-

lic until it is aromatic, about 20 seconds. Add the chilies and continue to stir-fry them until they are hot, about 30 seconds. Add the shrimp and stir-fry them until they are bright pink, about 2 minutes. Add the Kadai Sauce and the scallion. Stir-fry the shrimp until they are fully cooked, about 1 minute more. Season them with lemon juice and salt.

3. Serve at once.

Kadai Sauce

⅓ cup ghee (clarified butter) or corn oil
1 tbsp minced garlic
1 tbsp coriander seeds, toasted and coarsely pounded
3 dry red chilies, coarsely pounded in a mortar
2 red onions, finely chopped
1 (2 inch) piece ginger root, minced
3 green chilies, thinly sliced
1 lb plum tomatoes, peeled, seeded, and finely chopped
2 tsp kosher salt
1 tsp ground garam masala
1½ tsp dried fenugreek leaves
Kosher salt (optional)
Pinch of sugar (optional)

1. Heat the ghee in a sauté pan over medium-high heat. Add the garlic and sauté, stirring constantly, until just golden, about 30 seconds. Add the coriander seeds and red chilies and sauté until aromatic, 30 seconds. Add the onions and continue to stir-fry until they are golden brown, about 4 minutes.

2. Add the ginger, green chilies, and tomatoes. Reduce the heat to low and cook the ingredients until all the excess moisture has evaporated and the fat starts to rise to the surface, about 20 minutes.

3. Add the salt, garam masala, and fenugreek leaves and stir to combine. Season with salt and a pinch of sugar, if needed. The sauce is ready to use now or it can be cooled and stored in a covered container in the refrigerator for up to 3 days.

Spicy Shanghai Crawfish

This dish is popular in Shanghai. Leaving the shells on gives you the perfect excuse to eat with your fingers.

MAKES 4 TO 6 SERVINGS

2 lb live crawfish (or jumbo shrimp)
2 tbsp peanut oil
10 garlic cloves, peeled and lightly pounded
5 slices fresh ginger
8 dried red chilies
1 tbsp Sichuan peppercorns
2 tbsp soy sauce
1 tsp chicken bouillon cube
1 tbsp sugar
½ tsp sesame oil
½ cup water
Kosher salt, to taste

1. Soak live crawfish in salted cold water for half an hour. Rinse the crawfish with cold running water until they are thoroughly clean.
2. Heat the peanut oil in a wok or sauté pan over medium-high heat. Add the garlic, ginger, dried chilies, and Sichuan peppercorns and stir-fry until they are aromatic, about 1 minute. Add the crawfish (or shrimp) and stir-fry until the shells are bright red, about 5 minutes.
3. Add the soy sauce, bouillon cube, sugar, sesame oil, and water and stir to combine. Cover the wok or sauté and simmer for 5 minutes. Add salt to taste. Serve at once.

Katsuo-No-Tataki with Garlic Ginger Dipping Sauce

This fish dish topped with raw ginger, garlic, and scallions comes from Kochi, historically Japan's only garlic-loving province.

MAKES 4 SERVINGS

2 tsp vegetable oil
1 (12 oz) piece fresh bonito or tuna fillet, skin left on
½ cup scallions, thinly sliced into shreds
4 tsp grated ginger
2 tsp minced garlic
1 cup Garlic-Ginger Dipping Sauce (recipe follows)
2 cups julienned or shredded daikon
½ lemon, thinly sliced

1. Heat the oil in a frying pan over high heat. Add the bonito or tuna and sear the fish just until the flesh turns white, about 1 minute. Turn and cook the fish on the second side, about 1 minute. Immediately transfer the fish to a shallow dish and chill it in the refrigerator until cold, about 1 hour.

2. Combine ¼ cup of the scallions, half of the ginger and garlic, and ½ cup of the Garlic-Ginger Dipping Sauce in a small bowl. Pour the mixture over the chilled fish, turning to coat it evenly and patting the marinade into the fish with the flat side of your chef's knife. Cover and marinate the fish in the refrigerator at least 10 and up to 60 minutes.

3. To serve, make a bed on a chilled serving platter with the daikon. Slice the fish about ½ inch thick and arrange it over the daikon. Garnish the dish with the lemon slices and the remaining scallions, ginger, and garlic.

4. Serve chilled or at room temperature with the remaining Garlic-Ginger Dipping Sauce on the side.

Garlic-Ginger Dipping Sauce
MAKES 1 CUP

½ cup soy sauce

¼ cup rice wine vinegar

4 garlic cloves, minced

2 tbsp finely grated ginger

2 tbsp chopped scallions

2 tsp honey

1 tsp sesame oil

Place all of the ingredients in a jar and shake it well to combine them. This sauce can be stored in the refrigerator for up to 2 days.

VEGETARIAN

＿＿～＿＿

....

Good Fortune Stir-Fried Garlic Lettuce

In Cantonese, garlic is commonly known as *suin mei,* which can be translated as "plenty of money to count," and the word for lettuce (*saang choy*) sounds like "growing money"—so this recipe is a popular New Year's dish.

MAKES 4 SERVINGS

1 head iceberg lettuce, cored and separated into leaves

1½ tsp soy sauce

1½ tsp sesame oil

1 tsp rice wine or dry sherry

¾ tsp white sugar

¼ tsp ground white pepper

3 tbsp peanut or vegetable oil

3 medium garlic cloves, smashed and peeled

¼ tsp kosher salt

1. Wash the lettuce in several changes of cold water, breaking the leaves in half. Drain the lettuce thoroughly in a colander until it is dry to the touch.

2. To make the stir-fry sauce: Stir together the soy sauce, sesame oil, rice wine or sherry, sugar, and pepper in a small bowl until the sugar dissolves. Set aside.

3. Heat a wok or sauté pan over high heat. Add the peanut oil and garlic, and stir-fry the garlic until it is fragrant, 10 seconds. Add the lettuce and stir-fry 1 minute to coat the leaves. Add the salt and continue to stir-fry until the lettuce is just limp, 1 minute. Pour the sauce over the lettuce and stir-fry the lettuce until it is very hot and tender but still bright green, 1 minute more.

4. Serve at once on heated plates.

....

Eggplant in Garlic Sauce

For this Chinese dish, look for long, slender, Asian-style eggplant at the market rather than the larger, round, "globe" eggplant (it's less bitter).

MAKES 4 SERVINGS

3 tbsp peanut oil, divided

4 Chinese or Japanese eggplants (about 1½ lb), sliced into 1-inch-thick rounds

8 garlic cloves, minced

2 tsp chopped fresh ginger

2 tbsp soy sauce

1 tbsp hot bean paste

1 tbsp garlic chili paste, or to taste

1 tsp sugar

1 (8 oz) can sliced water chestnuts, drained

½ cup chicken stock or water

1 tbsp cornstarch

1 chopped scallion, for garnish

1 tbsp sesame oil, for garnish

1 tbsp toasted sesame seeds, for garnish

1. Heat about 2 tablespoons of the peanut oil in a wok or large sauté pan. Add the eggplant in batches and stir-fry the eggplant until it is golden, about 2 minutes. Transfer the eggplant to a plate and set it aside. Add more oil to the wok between batches and give the oil enough time to reheat before adding the remaining eggplant.

2. Return the wok or sauté pan to high heat. Add 1 tablespoon of peanut oil and the garlic and ginger. Stir-fry the garlic and ginger until they are aromatic, about 20 seconds. Add the soy sauce, bean paste, chili paste, and sugar. Stir-fry until blended and hot, about 20 seconds. Return the eggplant to the wok along with the water chestnuts, and stir-fry until the eggplant is coated, about 2 minutes.

3. Stir together the broth or water and the cornstarch and add the liquid to the wok. Simmer until the eggplant is very tender and the sauce is thickened, about 5 minutes.

4. Serve at once, garnished with the scallion, sesame oil, and sesame seeds.

....

Pondu Koszhambu

This spicy garlic and tamarind curry comes from Chettinad in Southern India. It is traditionally served with rice.

MAKES 4 SERVINGS

1 ball (ping-pong size) tamarind pulp

2 cups water

Kosher salt, as needed

1 tsp vegetable oil for skillet, plus 1 tbsp for pot or Dutch oven

½ tbsp channa dal (optional)

½ tsp black peppercorns

½ tsp coriander seeds

½ tsp cumin seeds

3 shallots, halved or quartered

4 garlic cloves, peeled and crushed, for spice paste; plus 20 garlic cloves, peeled and left whole for the curry

8 curry leaves, crumbled

2 dried red chilies (cayenne or Kashmiri), 1 chopped

½ tsp mustard seeds

½ tsp fenugreek seeds

6 shallots, halved or quartered depending on size

½ tomato, seeded and finely chopped

2 tsp brown sugar (optional)

½ tsp turmeric powder

½ tsp curry powder

¼ tsp chili powder

1 pinch asafoetida

4 cups steamed jasmine rice

1. Soak the tamarind in lightly salted warm water for 20 minutes. Strain the liquid from the tamarind through a sieve, pushing with a scraper or the back of a spoon to extract the pulp. Discard the fibers. You should have 2 cups of tamarind water. Set the water aside.

2. Heat 1 teaspoon of oil in a skillet. Add the channa dal (if using), peppercorns, coriander, cumin seeds, shallots, crushed garlic, curry leaves, and the chopped chili and toast the ingredients, stirring frequently, until they are aromatic, about 3 minutes. Immediately transfer them to a spice grinder or mortar and pestle and grind the ingredients into a paste. Set the paste aside.

3. Heat 1 tablespoon of oil in a Dutch oven or soup pot over medium-high heat. Add the whole chili, the remaining 4 curry leaves, mustard seeds, and fenugreek seeds until the seeds begin to pop, about 2 minutes. Add the garlic and shallots and sauté, stirring frequently, until they are lightly browned, about 6 minutes. Add the chopped tomato and sauté, stirring frequently, until the tomato has a sweet aroma, about 3 minutes. Stir in the brown sugar (if using), turmeric, curry powder, chili powder, and asafoetida

4. Stir the tamarind water into the curry. Stir the spice paste into the curry and return it to a simmer over medium heat. Simmer, stirring frequently, until the curry thickens, about 30 minutes.

5. Serve with hot steamed rice.

Tofu with Chimichurri Sauce on Garlic Toast

This recipe paints the blank canvas of tofu with the robust flavors of an Argentinian grill.

MAKES 4 SERVINGS

1 lb firm tofu

Chimichurri Sauce
2 cups chopped parsley
6 garlic cloves, minced
4 tbsp minced shallots
2 tsp minced oregano
1 tsp kosher salt
½ tsp freshly ground pepper
½ tsp red pepper flakes
½ cup extra-virgin olive oil, plus more as needed for Garlic Toast
3 tbsp sherry vinegar
3 tbsp lime juice

Garlic Toast
4 slices peasant or sourdough bread
2 garlic cloves, halved

1. Drain the tofu on several layers of paper towel. Top the tofu with additional paper towels and then add a weight to press excess moisture from the tofu. Let the tofu drain at least 30 minutes. Cut the tofu into 4 pieces.

2. To make the Chimichurri Sauce: Combine the parsley, garlic, shallots, oregano, salt, pepper, red pepper flakes, olive oil, vinegar, and lime juice in a bowl.

3. Place the tofu pieces in a dish or a zip-close bag. Add about 1 cup of the Chimichurri Sauce. Turn the tofu to coat it evenly, cover (if using a dish), and refrigerate the tofu for at least 3 and up to 12 hours.

4. Preheat a stovetop griddle or sauté pan over high heat. Add the tofu pieces and cook them on both sides until they are browned and heated through, about 2 minutes on each side.

5. To prepare the Garlic Toast: Brush the bread slices lightly with oil and rub them with the halved garlic cloves. Heat a second pan over medium-high heat. Add the bread and toast it on both sides until it is golden brown, about 2 minutes on each side.

6. Serve the tofu on the Garlic Toast, topped with additional Chimichurri Sauce.

....

Green Garlic Risotto

Green garlic is immature garlic, picked before the bulb has split into cloves. It's only available for a few weeks in the late spring and early summer. It has a mild, grassy flavor a bit like a strong scallion.

MAKES 4 SERVINGS

4 cups chicken or vegetable broth
1 cup dry white wine
2 tbsp olive oil
½ cup chopped green garlic, divided
1½ cups Arborio rice
2 tbsp butter
½ cup grated Parmesan
Kosher salt and freshly ground black pepper, to taste
Freshly squeezed lemon juice, to taste

1. Combine the broth and wine in a small saucepan and bring the liquid to a simmer over medium heat. Keep it hot throughout cooking.

2. Heat the olive oil in a large saucepan over medium heat. Add ¼ cup of the green garlic and sauté, stirring frequently, until it softens, about 2 minutes.

3. Add the rice and stir until it is coated with oil. Sauté the rice, stirring frequently, until the grains begin to change color and have a nutty aroma, about 2 minutes.

4. Add about 1½ cups of the broth-wine mixture to the rice and cook the rice, stirring constantly, until it absorbs the liquid. Add another 1½ cups of the broth-wine mixture and cook the rice until it absorbs the liquid. Add the remaining broth-wine mixture and cook the rice, stirring constantly, until it is fully cooked and tender and the risotto is creamy, about 18 minutes total.

5. Remove the saucepan from the heat and stir in the butter, Parmesan, and remaining green garlic. Season the rice with salt, black pepper, and a squeeze of fresh lemon juice. Serve at once in heated soup plates.

Roasted Garlic Soufflé

The base for this soufflé, known to chefs as a béchamel, can be prepared up to 4 days ahead of time. The milk for the béchamel is infused with the flavors of raw garlic, fresh thyme, and black peppercorns for a robust flavor. Serve this soufflé for a light supper, paired with crusty bread, some salad, and a glass of wine.

MAKES 4 SERVINGS

Butter, to prepare the baking dish
2½ cups whole milk
3 garlic cloves, peeled and crushed
3 sprigs fresh thyme
1 tsp black peppercorns
6 tbsp unsalted butter, plus more as needed for coating soufflé dish
5 tbsp all-purpose flour

4 large egg yolks

3 heads garlic, roasted and pureed

1½ cups grated Parmesan, plus 4 tsp for sprinkling soufflé dish

1 cup (5 oz) crumbled goat cheese

1 teaspoon fresh thyme leaves

Few grains freshly grated nutmeg

8 egg whites

1. Preheat the oven to 400°F and arrange a rack in the middle of the oven. Brush a 2-quart soufflé dish with butter and coat it with about four teaspoons of Parmesan. Set the dish aside.

2. Combine the milk, garlic cloves, thyme sprigs, and peppercorns in a saucepan and bring the mixture to a simmer over medium heat. Immediately remove the pan from the heat and let the milk steep for at least 20 minutes.

3. Heat the butter in a saucepan over medium heat until it has melted. Stir in the flour to make a smooth paste, and then cook it, stirring constantly, until it turns golden and has a light, nutty aroma, about 4 minutes. Strain the milk into the butter-flour mixture gradually and whisk to remove any lumps. Bring the mixture back to a simmer over medium-low heat and simmer, stirring frequently, until it is thickened and very smooth, about 10 minutes.

4. Pour the sauce into a bowl and whisk in the egg yolks one at a time. Add the roasted garlic puree, Parmesan, goat cheese, thyme leaves, and nutmeg, and fold the ingredients together until they are evenly blended.

5. Whip the egg whites with an electric mixer or by hand to medium peaks. Fold the egg whites into the cheese mixture in three separate additions. Spoon the soufflé batter into the prepared dish. Bake it until the soufflé is puffed and golden brown on the top and sides, 20 to 25 minutes.

6. Serve the soufflé at once by scooping out portions onto heated plates.

SIDE DISHES

⌒

Hasselback Potatoes

These accordion-cut potatoes are named for Hasselbacken, the restaurant in Stockholm that first served them. The cutting technique calls for two chopsticks arranged along the sides of the potato. The chopsticks prevent the knife blade from cutting all the way through the potato as you slice, leaving the bottom ⅛ inch still intact.

MAKES 4 SERVINGS

4 medium russet potatoes
4 garlic cloves, thinly sliced
2 tbsp olive oil
Coarse sea salt and freshly ground black pepper, as needed

1. Preheat the oven to 425°F. Put each potato on a chopping board, flat side down between two chopsticks. Start from one end of the potato and cut almost all the way through, at about ⅛ inch intervals.
2. Arrange the potatoes in a baking dish and press down on them to spread out the slices. Insert the sliced garlic in the slits. Then

drizzle the potatoes with olive oil and sprinkle them with sea salt and pepper.

3. Cover the dish and bake the potatoes until the potatoes are tender, 45 to 50 minutes. Remove the cover and bake the potatoes until they are golden on top, another 10 minutes.

....

Garlic Mashed Potatoes

These magnificent potatoes, based upon the classic recipe from Julia Child's *Mastering the Art of French Cooking,* are a world removed from standard whipped potatoes. The extra step of preparing a garlic cream is worth the effort.

MAKES 8 SERVINGS

2½ lb baking potatoes, peeled and quartered
Kosher salt, to taste, divided
¼ cup butter, softened
Garlic Cream (recipe follows)
¼ cup heavy cream, heated, as needed
Freshly ground pepper, to taste
¼ cup minced parsley

1. Make the Garlic Cream (recipe follows).
2. Place the potatoes in a deep pot and add enough cold water to cover them by about 1 inch. Add salt to taste and bring the potatoes to a simmer over medium heat. Simmer until the potatoes are very tender, about 20 minutes. Drain the potatoes in a colander and then return them to the pot. Let the potatoes dry for 1 or 2 minutes over low heat.
3. Pull the pot from the heat and beat the potatoes using a wooden spoon or a potato masher. Stir in the butter, Garlic Cream, and enough heavy cream to reach the desired consistency. Add salt and

pepper to taste. Beat in the minced parsley and serve the mashed potatoes at once.

Garlic Cream
4 tbsp butter
30 garlic cloves, blanched and peeled
2 tbsp all-purpose flour
1 cup milk, heated
Kosher salt and ground white pepper, as needed

Melt the butter in a small heavy-bottomed saucepan over medium heat. Add the garlic, cover, and cook over low heat, stirring occasionally, until the garlic is very soft and tender but not browned, about 20 minutes. Add the flour and stir to make a smooth paste. Cook the paste over low heat until the flour smells toasty, about 2 minutes. Stir in the milk, salt, and pepper, whisking to remove any lumps. Simmer, stirring constantly, until the sauce is thickened, about 3 minutes. Let the sauce cool for 10 minutes before pureeing it in a food processor or with a hand blender. Keep warm.

....

Mamaliga
(Polenta)

Polenta served with a garlic sauce is a traditional meal in Romania and Moldova. Telemea is a traditional cheese from the region, but you can replace it with feta.

Mujdei Sauce (recipe follows)
3½ cups water
1½ tsp kosher salt
2 tbsp butter
1 cup coarse yellow cornmeal
½ cup crumbled telemea or feta cheese (optional), to serve
2 tbsp minced chives, thyme, or marjoram, to serve

1. Make the Mujdei Sauce (see below).
2. Bring the water to a rolling boil in a deep pot. Add the salt and butter. Pour the cornmeal into the boiling water in a very thin stream while stirring constantly with a wooden spoon. Continue to cook the cornmeal, stirring frequently, until the Mamaglia is tender and creamy, 35 to 40 minutes.
3. Serve the Mamaglia at once in heated soup plates topped with the Mujdei Sauce, telemea or feta, and herbs.

Mujdei Sauce

1 head garlic, cloves separated and peeled
1 tsp kosher salt
2 tbsp canola oil
½ cup sour cream
Freshly ground black pepper, to taste

1. Put the garlic in a mortar with the salt and crush it to a paste. Stir together the garlic paste and oil in a small bowl until the mixture is blended and thickened, about 3 minutes.
2. Stir in the sour cream and season it generously with black pepper. The sauce is ready to serve now or store in a covered container in the refrigerator for up to 2 days.

....

Broccoli Raab with Toasted Garlic and Anchovies

Broccoli raab has a slight bitterness that is a perfect foil for the garlic and anchovies in this sauté. The flavor combination works well with other bitter cooking greens, including escarole and kale.

MAKES 4 SERVINGS

1½ lb broccoli raab, stems peeled
3 tbsp olive oil
8 garlic cloves, peeled and thinly sliced

3 anchovy fillets, drained and chopped

¼ tsp red pepper flakes, or more to taste

Kosher salt and freshly ground black pepper, to taste

1. Bring a large pot of salted water to a rolling boil over high heat. Add the broccoli raab and cook it until it is bright green and barely tender, about 3 minutes. Immediately transfer it to a colander and rinse it with cold water to stop the cooking. Let the broccoli raab drain well.

2. Combine the oil and garlic in a sauté pan and heat it gently over medium heat until the garlic is golden brown and crisp. Lift the toasted garlic from the oil and set it aside.

3. Add the anchovy fillets and red pepper flakes and sauté, smashing the anchovy with the back of a spoon until it dissolves. Add the drained broccoli raab and continue to sauté, tossing or stirring until it is coated evenly and very hot, 2 to 3 minutes. Season the dish with salt and pepper.

4. Serve the broccoli raab at once, topped with the toasted garlic.

....

Garlicky Collard Greens and Beans

An Americanized version of a classic Italian dish, this is a perfect side for fried chicken or chicken-fried steak. Serve it as a main dish on a bed of grits.

MAKES 4 SERVINGS

1½ lb collard greens, chopped

2 tbsp olive oil

2 slices pancetta, minced

6 garlic cloves, minced

1½ cups cooked white beans, drained and rinsed

½ cup chicken broth or water

Kosher salt and freshly ground black pepper, to taste

1. Bring a large pot of salted water to a rolling boil over high heat. Add the collard greens and stir to submerge them. Cook the greens until they are bright green and barely tender, about 3 minutes. Immediately transfer them to a colander and rinse them with cold water to stop the cooking. Let the collard greens drain well.

2. Combine the oil and pancetta in a sauté pan and heat it gently over medium heat until the pancetta bits are crisp. Lift the pancetta bits from the oil and set them aside.

3. Add the garlic to the hot oil and sauté, stirring constantly, until the garlic is aromatic, about 1 minute. Add the collard greens and continue to sauté, tossing or stirring until the collard greens are coated with oil and very hot, about 3 minutes. Add the beans and the broth or water, and simmer the collard greens until they are tender and the broth has nearly cooked away. Season the dish with salt and pepper and serve at once.

DESSERT

~~~

Garlic-Pecan Brittle

The trick to making brittle is to have everything ready and at the right temperature before you start cooking. Cooked sugar is always extremely hot, so be sure to protect your hands and arms, and always pour the molten liquid away from you. This brittle makes a great confection on its own, dipped in chocolate, or sprinkled over ice cream. Try it in the Garlic Brittle and Chocolate Chip Cookies too (page 234).

MAKES ABOUT 12 OUNCES

½ cup garlic cloves, blanched and peeled
1 cup sugar
¼ cup corn syrup
2 tbsp butter, room temperature
1 tsp vanilla
¼ tsp kosher salt
1 cup pecans, toasted and chopped

1. Line a baking sheet with a nonstick silicone baking mat, parchment, or wax paper.

2. Chop the garlic coarsely and set it aside.

3. Combine the sugar and corn syrup in a large, heavy-bottomed saucepan over medium heat. Stir until the sugar dissolves, about 5 minutes. Continue to boil the mixture until it reaches 300°F (hard crack stage) on a candy thermometer and is a rich golden brown.

4. Immediately remove the mixture from the heat and add the butter, vanilla, and salt, stirring until the butter melts and is completely emulsified into the sugar. Add the garlic and pecans and stir to coat them completely.

5. Working quickly and carefully, scrape the hot mixture onto the prepared baking sheet. Tilt the pan so it flows into an even layer. After it has cooled for a minute or two, use a metal or silicon spatula to spread it into an even layer. Let the brittle cool completely, at least 1 hour, and then break it into chunks.

....

Garlic Brittle and Chocolate Chip Cookies

These cookies don't scream "garlic"; instead, the flavor comes on gradually, making the garlic a mystery ingredient. The extra sugar from the brittle chunks makes these cookies spread a bit, so be sure to leave plenty of room between them as they bake.

MAKES 2¹/₂ DOZEN COOKIES

2½ cups all-purpose flour
½ tsp baking soda
1 tsp kosher salt
1 cup (2 sticks) butter, softened
¾ cup granulated sugar
¾ cup packed brown sugar
1 tsp vanilla extract
2 large eggs
2 cups semi-sweet chocolate chips
1 cup chopped Garlic-Pecan Brittle (page 233)

1. Preheat the oven to 375°F.
2. Whisk together the flour, baking soda, and salt in a bowl.
3. Beat the butter, granulated sugar, brown sugar, and vanilla extract in a stand mixer with the paddle attachment on medium speed until the ingredients are creamy, about 2 minutes. Add the eggs one at a time, beating well after each addition and scraping down the bowl to blend them evenly.
4. By hand or on low speed, blend in the flour mixture. Stir in the chocolate chips and Garlic-Pecan Brittle.
5. Drop the batter by rounded tablespoon onto ungreased baking sheets, leaving at least 3 inches between the cookies.
6. Bake the cookies until golden brown, 10 to 12 minutes. Cool the cookies on the baking sheets for 2 minutes before transferring them to wire racks to cool completely.

....

Roasted Garlic Chocolate Truffles

Truffles are an easy confection to make. Adding roasted garlic to a traditional ganache made of cream and chocolate gives these truffles a decided twist. Before serving, give them a little time to warm up after you take them from the refrigerator for the richest aroma and texture.

MAKES 36 TRUFFLES

3 oz bittersweet chocolate, chopped
3 oz semisweet chocolate, chopped
1 cup heavy cream
4 tbsp unsalted butter
1 head garlic, roasted and pureed
Powdered unsweetened cocoa, for rolling the truffles

1. Place the chopped chocolates in a medium-sized bowl.
2. Bring the cream to a simmer in a small, heavy saucepan, and then pour the cream over the chocolate. Let the mixture sit for 2 or 3

minutes and then stir the chocolate until it is melted into the cream. Stir in the butter and the garlic puree. Cover and cool the mixture in the refrigerator until it is very firm, at least 40 minutes and up to 24 hours.

3. Line a baking sheet with parchment paper and sift a few table-spoons of cocoa onto the paper.

4. Scoop the truffle mixture into 1 tablespoon pieces and roll it into balls between the palms of your hands. Transfer the balls to the cocoa-lined baking sheet. When all the truffles are shaped, sift additional cocoa over the truffles and gently roll the truffles to coat all sides. Keep the truffles refrigerated until ready to serve.

....

Roasted Garlic and Coffee Ice Cream

Heston Blumenthal, chef of The Fat Duck, is known for his molecular gastronomy. He also pioneered flavor pairing of complementary but unique ingredients. One of his pairings is garlic and coffee. This roasted garlic ice cream with a coffee-garlic swirl was inspired by that pairing.

MAKES 1 QUART

2 cups cream
1 cup milk
2 heads garlic, roasted and pureed
¼ cup dark roast coffee beans
2 tbsp honey
4 large egg yolks
½ cup sugar
1 tsp vanilla extract
1 cup coarsely chopped Garlic-Coffee Brittle (see Note)

1. Combine the cream, milk, garlic, coffee, and honey in saucepan over medium heat. Bring the mixture to a simmer, and then remove it

from the heat, cover it, and let it steep for 1 hour. Strain the mixture into a clean saucepan and return it to a simmer, over medium heat.

2. Mix the egg yolks, sugar, and vanilla in bowl. Whisk a ladleful of the garlic-cream mixture into the yolk mixture until smooth. Return this mixture to the saucepan and simmer it until it has thickened enough to coat the back of a wooden spoon, about 6 minutes. Strain the mixture through a wire-mesh sieve into a bowl. Cool it to room temperature and then refrigerate it in a covered container for at least 8 and up to 24 hours.

3. Freeze the mixture in an ice cream maker according to the manufacturer's directions. Transfer the soft frozen ice cream to a bowl and fold in the Garlic-Coffee Brittle. Pack the ice cream into freezer containers and let the ice cream ripen in the freezer for at least 3 hours before serving. If the ice cream has been frozen longer than 6 hours, transfer it to the refrigerator for 30 minutes before serving.

NOTE

To make a Garlic-Coffee Brittle for ice cream, follow the recipe for Garlic-Pecan Brittle (page 233), but replace the pecans with ⅓ cup coarsely cracked dark roast or espresso coffee beans.

....

Roasted Garlic Crème Brûlée

Roasted garlic adds a rich, toasty flavor to the custard that is perfectly set off by the burnt sugar crust. A perfect brûlée should shatter when you crack it open with the back of a spoon.

MAKES 5 SERVINGS

2 cups heavy cream
5 egg yolks
2 tbsp sugar, plus 10 tsp for brûlée
2 heads garlic, roasted and pureed
½ tsp kosher salt

1. Preheat the oven to 275°F. Arrange 5 brûlée dishes or custard cups in a deep baking dish.

2. Whisk together the cream, egg yolks, and 2 tablespoons of sugar in a bowl until the sugar dissolves and the mixture is smooth. Add the garlic and salt and blend well. Strain the mixture into the brûlée dishes or custard cups, filling them evenly. Set the dish on a rack in the oven. Add boiling water to the baking dish to a depth of 1 inch.

3. Bake the custards until they are thickened and almost set (the center should be set but still wobble slightly when you shake the cup a little), about 40 minutes. Cool the custards to room temperature and then cover and refrigerate them for at least 8 and up to 24 hours.

4. Preheat the broiler to high. Sprinkle 2 teaspoons of sugar evenly over each custard and set the dishes or cups on a broiler pan or baking sheet. Broil the custards until the sugar turns dark brown and forms a crisp crust, about 6 minutes. Serve at once.

HISTORICAL RECIPES

⁓

Sumerian tablets, written in cuneiform on clay tablets over 3,500 years ago, first began to come to light starting in the 1850s. At first, it was surmised that these tablets were pharmaceutical formulas. However, the French Assyriologist Jean Bottéro, an accomplished chef, managed to decode three clay tablets, written in Akkadian around 1700 B.C.E., and found that they were recipes for a range of foods from gazelles to birds to cereals to turnips (*The Oldest Cuisine in the World: Cooking in Mesopotamia* [University of Chicago Press, 2004]). Bottéro proclaimed the food "fit only for his worst enemies," but others who have sampled re-creations of some of the dishes were more impressed.

Translating the recipes into something a modern cook might try is challenging for several reasons. The tablets are cracked in some places and discolored in others, leaving gaps and illegible portions in the text. Brackets in the recipes reflect the translator's best guess as to what the missing words might be. Another difficulty is the fact that many of the ingredients listed no longer exist. One ingredient in particular, blood, was used to enrich and thicken sauces; it gives foods a deep, almost black color and a distinct flavor that most modern eaters may never encounter.

We do know that Sumerians enjoyed a range of spices, a wide array of onion family members including leeks, as well as plenty of garlic. In that spirit, the recipes that follow Bottéro's translations here are meant to approximate the flavors and textures of what some have called the world's most ancient cuisine.

....

Goat Stew with Fat, Garlic, Onions, Sour Milk, and Blood

From the Sumerian: *Singe head, legs, and tail over flame* [before putting in pot]. *Meat* [in addition to kid] *is needed,* [preferably mutton to sharpen the flavor]. *Bring water to boil. Throw in fat. Squeeze onion, samîdu* [a plant probably of the onion family, and] *garlic* [to extract juices, add to pot with] *blood and soured milk.* [Add] *an equal amount of raw šuhutinnu* [another plant probably of the onion family] *and serve.*

Here is an adaptation: If you prefer, you can tie the clove and peppercorns into a small piece of cheesecloth or put them in a tea ball, to make it easier to take them out.

MAKES 4 TO 6 SERVINGS

2½ lb goat meat, cut into 3-inch pieces

Kosher salt and freshly ground black pepper, to taste

5 tbsp rendered lamb or goat fat, or lard

1 large onion, finely chopped

2 leeks, white and light green portions, chopped

16 garlic cloves, minced, divided

2 carrots, finely chopped

2 tsp tomato puree

Broth or water, as needed

2 cloves

¼ tsp black peppercorns

1 cup pork blood (see Note)

1 cup Greek-style yogurt

1. Season the goat meat with salt and pepper.
2. Heat the fat or lard in a Dutch oven or flameproof casserole over medium-high heat. Brown the goat on all sides, turning as necessary to cook the meat evenly, until it is dark brown, about 10 minutes. Transfer the meat to a plate and set it aside.
3. Add the onion, leeks, 12 of the garlic cloves, and carrots to the pot and sauté, stirring frequently, until the onions and garlic are golden, about 8 minutes. Add the tomato puree and stir to combine. Cook the mixture over medium heat until the tomato paste darkens and smells sweet, about 2 minutes. Return the goat meat to the pot and add enough broth or water to cover it. Add the cloves and peppercorns and simmer, partially covered, until the goat is very tender, about 1½ to 2 hours. Just before serving, stir in the blood and yogurt and return the mixture to a simmer until the sauce thickens, 3 to 4 minutes. Serve at once.

NOTE

It can be difficult to find blood for cooking, but if there are butchers in your area, you may be able to purchase it from them. Blood is extremely perishable, however, so it should be cooked as soon as possible. If the butcher has not added an anticoagulant to the blood, stir in about 1 teaspoon of red wine vinegar to each cup of blood.

....

Bird Stew with Garlic, Onions, Malt Cake, and Milk

From the Sumerian: [Besides the tărru birds, which may have been pigeon, quail or partridge,] *meat from a fresh leg of mutton is needed. Boil the water, throw fat in. Dress the tărru* [and place in pot]. *Add coarse salt as needed.* [Add] *hulled cake of malt. Squeeze onions, samîdu, leek, garlic* [together], *and* [add to pot along with] *milk. After* [cooking and] *cutting up the tărru, plunge them* [to braise] *in stock* [from the pot]. *Then place them back in the pot* [in order to finish cooking]. *To be brought out for carving.*

3 tbsp rendered chicken or lamb fat, or olive oil

6 quail, trussed

1 leek, cleaned and thickly sliced

1 onion, coarsely chopped

1 shallot, coarsely chopped

8 garlic cloves, coarsely chopped

2 cups milk

1 tbsp vinegar

Barley Cakes

2 cups barley flour

¼ cup rendered chicken or lamb fat, or vegetable shortening

1 tsp kosher salt

Broth or water, as needed

1. Preheat the oven to 325°F.
2. Heat the fat or oil in a Dutch oven or flameproof casserole over medium-high heat. Add the quail and sear them on all sides, turning as necessary, until they are golden brown, about 8 minutes. Transfer the quail to a plate. Add the leek, onion, shallot, and garlic to the pot and sauté, stirring frequently, until the onion is tender and golden brown, about 8 minutes.
3. Spread the sautéed vegetables in an even layer to make a bed. Return the quail, arranging them on the vegetables. Add the milk and vinegar and bring the mixture to a simmer. Cover the Dutch oven or casserole and place it in the oven. Braise the quail until they are tender and cooked through, about 40 minutes.
4. For the barley cakes: Mix together ¼ cup of the barley flour, the fat, and salt, then gradually stir in enough of the braising liquid from the quail to make a pliable but fairly stiff dough. Divide the dough into 6 equal pieces. Roll each piece into a 6-inch circle.
5. Heat a cast-iron skillet or griddle over medium-high heat and coat

it lightly with a little additional fat. Working with one flatbread at a time, cook it in the hot skillet until it is cooked through and lightly charred, about 1 minute on each side. Add more fat or oil to the pan if necessary. Wrap the barley cakes in a clean cloth and keep warm.

6. To serve, place a quail on top of the flatbreads and spoon the braising liquid, including the vegetables, over the quail. Serve at once.

....

Braised Turnips with Fat, Cumin, Coriander, Leek, and Garlic

From the Sumerian: *Meat is not needed. Boil water. Throw fat in.* [Add] *onion, dorsal thorn* [name of unknown plant used as seasoning], *coriander, cumin and kanafl* [a legume]. *Squeeze leek and garlic and spread* [juice] *on dish. Add onion and mint.*

MAKES 6 SERVINGS

2 leeks, divided
4 turnips, peeled and quartered
16 garlic cloves, peeled but left whole, divided
1 onion, coarsely chopped
½ cup lentils
1 (3 oz) piece salt pork or slab bacon, left in one piece
1½ teaspoon coriander seeds
1 tsp cumin seeds
1 bunch mint, leaves coarsely chopped
Kosher salt and freshly ground black pepper, to taste

1. Trim 1 leek and slice the white and light green portions into rounds. Combine the sliced leeks turnips, 12 whole garlic cloves, the onion, lentils, salt pork or slab bacon, coriander seeds, and cumin seeds in a stockpot. Add enough cold water to just cover the turnips. Bring the water to boil, then reduce the heat and simmer,

partially covered, until the turnips and garlic are tender, about 40 minutes.

2. Mince the tender white portion of the second leek and the remaining 4 garlic cloves in a food processor or mortar and pestle. Add the mint and continue to mince or process the mixture to an even paste. Add some of the cooking liquid from the turnips to help grind the mixture evenly if necessary.

3. Stir the leek-garlic-mint puree into the turnips and lentils. Season with salt and pepper and serve at once.

....

Moretum

Moretum is an ancient garlic cheese dish eaten by shepherds and described by Virgil in a poem of the same name. The recipe below was adapted from *GodeCookery,* a website devoted to historical cooking (www.godecookery.com). The exact quantity of garlic that the ancients might have used is a matter of debate. This recipe calls for 8 cloves, an excellent starting place that you can modify to suit your own preference and tolerance!

> The reeking garlic with the pestle breaks,
> Then everything he equally doth rub
> th' mingled juice. His hand in circles move:
> . . .
> A single colour, not entirely green
> Because the milky fragments this forbid,
> Nor showing white as from the milk because
> That colour's altered by so many herbs.
> . . .
> A little of his scanty vinegar,
> And mixes once again his handiwork,
> And mixed withdraws it: then with fingers twain
> Round all the mortar doth he go at last

And into one coherent ball doth bring
The diff'rent portions, that it may the name
And likeness of a finished salad fit.

—*from "Moretum," or "The Salad"*

8 garlic cloves, finely minced
2 celery stalks, finely minced
½ bunch cilantro, leaves only
½ bunch lovage, leaves only (optional)
4 oz fresh feta cheese, crumbled
2 tbsp olive oil
2 tbsp white wine vinegar

Chop the garlic, celery, cilantro, and lovage (if using) in a mortar and pestle or a food processor into an even but coarse paste. Add the feta cheese, olive oil, and vinegar. Pound or process the ingredients into a smooth paste. Pack the mixture into a covered crock or serving dish and refrigerate it at least 2 and up to 24 hours before serving.

Lièvre à la Royale

Lièvre à la Royale is hare braised in red wine with 20 cloves of garlic and 40 shallots. Many call it the mythic dish of France, though it was regarded as "a rather mediocre hash that's strongly flavored with shallots and garlic" by Prosper Montagne who wrote *Larousse gastronomique*. Not everyone agreed with him, of course. Elizabeth David's version in *A Book of Mediterranean Food* is the inspiration for this rendition.

1 rabbit, with liver and heart reserved
Salt and pepper, to taste
4 thick slices unsmoked bacon

3 tbsp goose or duck fat

2 onions, chopped

1 carrot

20 garlic cloves, peeled but left whole

8 shallots, peeled but left whole

⅓ cup red wine vinegar

1 cup dry red wine

1. Trim the rabbit and season it well with salt and pepper. Wrap the rabbit loin with the bacon slices to keep the loin covered as the rabbit braises.

2. Heat the goose or duck fat in a Dutch oven or flameproof casserole over medium-high heat. Add the onions and carrot and sauté, stirring frequently, until the onions are a light golden brown, about 10 minutes. Add the garlic and shallots and continue to sauté until coated with oil and a light golden, 3 to 4 minutes. Place the rabbit on top of the vegetables and pour in the vinegar and wine. Cover the pot, and braise the meat in the oven until very tender, 2½ to 3 hours.

3. To finish the dish, remove the rabbit and keep the meat warm. Place the Dutch oven or casserole over medium heat and return the sauce to a simmer. Mince the liver and heart very fine and add them to the sauce. Continue to simmer the sauce until it is thickened and flavorful, about 10 minutes. Cut the rabbit into portions and return it to the sauce to reheat it.

4. Serve the rabbit with the sauce in heated plates.

Acknowledgments

This book is dedicated to the memory of my brilliant and funny mother, who taught me how to cook and made sure I never used a garlic press because Craig Claiborne said it made the garlic bitter. I miss you, Mom.

Special thanks go out to Abigail Koons, my smart and delightful agent, and to my gracious and talented editor Rochelle Bourgault and her wonderful team at Roost Books. The recipes were developed by Mary Deir Donovan, a knowledgeable and enthusiastic collaborator who I can't wait to work with again. I hope you enjoy her delicious, garlicky recipes as I much as I do.

This book is a tribute to the many garlic farmers, educators, writers, and chefs I've had the privilege to meet and learn from. You are an inspiring group of fascinating and often fragrant people.

Bibliography

Aaron, Chester. *Garlic is Life: A Memoir with Recipes.* Berkeley, Calif.: Ten Speed Press, 1996.

Adema, Pauline. *Garlic Capital of the World: Gilroy, Garlic, and the Making of a Festive Foodscape.* Jackson, Miss.: University Press of Mississippi, 2009.

Anderson, Bob. *Gourmet Garlic Gardens: A Garlic Information Center*, 1997–2014, www.gourmetgarlicgardens.com.

Block, Eric. *Garlic and Other Alliums: The Lore and the Science.* Cambridge, U.K.: The Royal Society of Chemistry, 2010.

Bourdain, Anthony. *Kitchen Confidential: Adventures in the Culinary Underbelly.* New York: Harper Collins, 2001.

Clickner, Tricia. *A Miscellany of Garlic: From Paying Off Pyramids and Scaring Away Tigers to Inspiring Courage and Curing Hiccups, the Unusual Power Behind the World's Most Humble Vegetable.* Avon, Mass.: F+W Media, 2012.

David, Elizabeth. *French Country Cooking.* London: Penguin U.K., 2001.

_____. *Is There a Nutmeg in the House?: Essays on Practical Cooking with More Than 150 Recipes.* New York: Viking Penguin Books, 2001.

Edwards, Natasha. *The Garlic Farm Cookbook.* The Isle of Wight, U.K.: The Garlic Press, 2010.

_____. *Garlic: The Mighty Bulb.* London: Kyle Books, 2012.

Engeland, Ron L. *Growing Great Garlic: The Definitive Guide for Organic Gardeners and Small Farmers.* Okanogan, Wash.: Filaree Productions, 1991.

Fulder, Stephen. *The Garlic Book: Nature's Powerful Healer.* New York: Avery, 1997.

Griffith, Fred and Linda Griffith. *Garlic, Garlic, Garlic: More than 200 Exceptional Recipes from the World's Most Indispensable Ingredients.* Boston: Houghton Mifflin Harcourt, 1998.

Harris, Lloyd J. *Book of Garlic.* New York: Holt, Rinehart, and Winston, 1975.

Hicks, Alexandra. "The Mystique of Garlic: History, Uses, Superstitions, and Scientific Revelations" in *Proceedings from the Oxford Symposium on Food and Cookery, 1984-1985; Cookery: Science, Lore and Books*. London: Oxford University Press, 1986.

Hobbs, Christopher. "Garlic: The Pungent Panacea" in *Pharmacy in History*. School of Pharmacy, University of Wisconsin, Madison, 1998, https://pharmacy.wisc.edu.

Lake, Alan. *The Garlic Manifesto: An Idiosyncratic View of Garlic through the Ages*. Jazzfood Press, 2014.

Meredith, Ted Jordan. *The Complete Book of Garlic: A Guide for Gardeners, Growers, and Serious Cooks*. Portland, Oreg.: Timber Press, 2008.

Nekola, Jeff. *Heirloom Vegetable Archive: Garlic*, 2010, http://sev.lternet.edu/~jnekola/Heirloom/garlicA.htm.

O'Brien, Paul. "Garlic in Traditional Chinese Medicine," Spezzatino.com.

Olney, Richard. *Simple French Food*. Boston: Houghton Mifflin Harcourt, 2014.

Perrottet, Tony. *The Naked Olympics: The True Story of the Ancient Games*. New York: Random House Trade Paperbacks, 2004.

Renoux, Victoria. *For the Love of Garlic: The Complete Guide to Garlic Cuisine*. Garden City Park, N.Y.: Square One Publishers, 2005.

Rivlin, Richard S. "Historical Perspective on the Use of Garlic," *The Journal of Nutrition* 131, no. 3. The American Society for Nutritional Sciences, 2001.

Stern, David and Bob Dunkel. *The Garlic Press Newsletter*. New York: Garlic Seed Foundation, 1987–2013.

Swenson, John. "Stalking Alliums Along the Silk Road: 1989 US-Soviet Expedition," *Repast: Quarterly Newsletter of the Culinary Historians of Ann Arbor*, winter 2005. Culinary Historians of Ann Arbor, 2005.

Index

mashed potatoes, 2, 62, 228–29
mashing garlic, 122
Massaman Lamb Curry, 195–96
Mastering the Art of French Cooking
(Child and Beck), 2, 62, 191, 228
matzo meal, 177–78
Medical School at Salerno, 21
medicinal uses of garlic
  allergy treatment, 38
  Alzheimer's treatment, 33, 36
  antibacterial uses, 30
  anticoagulant uses, 30, 33–34
  anti-inflammatory properties, 38
  antimicrobial uses, 30
  antioxidants, 36
  arthritis treatment, 38
  asthma treatment, 38
  Ayurvedic tradition, 1, 18–19, 50
  blood circulation, 40
  blood pressure, 51
  cancer prevention and treatment,
    11–12, 16–17, 37–38
  cardiovascular health, 14–15,
    18–19, 30, 33–34
  chelation therapy, 39
  cholesterol lowering, 34
  cold remedy, 29
  digestive health, 18–19, 31
  in Egypt, 12–13
  in England, 22–23
  food poisoning treatment, 32
  German traditions, 21–22
  heavy metal toxicity treatment, 39
  herpes treatment, 31
  impotence treatment, 17, 40
  influenza treatment, 28–29, 31
  Islamic traditions, 20, 22
  in Italy, 22
  leprosy and, 21
  macrophage stimulation, 34–35
  in medieval Europe, 20–22
  modern research on, 31–42
  natural killer (NK) cell
    stimulation, 34–35

Parkinson's disease treatment, 33,
  36
pneumonia treatment, 31
precautions, 41–42
pregnancy, 36–37
prostate health, 40
Siddha medical tradition, 18
sterility, 12–13
T-helper cell stimulation, 34–35
Traditional Chinese Medicine, 1,
  16–17, 47–48
Unani medical tradition, 19–20
weight control, 38
The Medicine of the Prophet (Islamic
  text), 20
medieval Europe, 20–21, 52–56, 74
Mesopotamia. *See also* Middle
  Eastern cuisine: Sumerian recipes
Metechi garlic, 102
Meyer, Stephenie, 85–86
Middle East, 51. *See also* Egypt;
  Islamic traditions; Middle
  Eastern cuisine
Middle Eastern cuisine, 51–52
  Acii Esme (Turkish yogurt sauce), 127
  Harissa (North African chili
    sauce), 128–29
  hummus, 125–26
  Pipelchuma (Libyan hot pepper
    garlic sauce), 133–34
  Roasted Garlic and Quinoa Salad,
    165–66
  Sumerian recipes, 44, 239–44
  Zaalouk (Moroccan roasted
    vegetables), 161–62
  Zhoug (Yemeni chutney), 135–36
milk, 19, 69
mincing garlic, 122
miso, 138
Mohammed, the Prophet, 20, 22,
  71–72
Mom's Oklahoma Rocambole, 95
monasteries, Christian, 20–21, 52
moral depravity, 71–74. *See also*

About the Author

Photograph © Alex Kaplan

Robin Cherry is a writer and historian with a passion for travel, food, and popular culture. She is the author of *Catalog: The Illustrated History of Mail Order Shopping* and has written for *The Atlantic*, *National Geographic Traveler*, *Dwell*, *Salon*, and many other publications and websites. As a travel writer, she has visited many of the places featured in *Garlic, an Edible Biography*, including Europe, Asia, the Middle East, and Gilroy, California. She lives in New York's Hudson Valley, home of what she believes is the world's best garlic festival.